Education and Responsibility

Education
and
Responsibility

TUNIS ROMEIN

University of Kentucky Press

LEXINGTON

Publication of this book is possible partly
by reason of a grant from the
Margaret Voorhies Haggin Trust
established in memory of her husband
James Ben Ali Haggin

To Sally and the children

Acknowledgments

UNIVERSITY of Kentucky Professors Ellis Hartford, John Kuiper, and Jesse DeBoer were valuable advisors and critics throughout the writing of the manuscript. In addition, important help was given by other members of the University of Kentucky faculty: Harold P. Adams, Herbert Sorenson, C. W. Hackensmith, John Melzer, Donald Fryxell (now at Augustana College), and Amry Vandenbosch; and also by Velorus Martz, professor emeritus at Indiana University.

I also sincerely appreciate the encouragement of Herman E. Spivey, dean of the University of Kentucky Graduate School, and Frank Dickey, dean of the University of Kentucky College of Education.

TUNIS ROMEIN

Mitchell College
November 15, 1954

Contents

IV

EDUCATION, THE COMMUNITY, AND CHRISTIAN FAITH

Introduction

SIMPLY speaking, responsibility is answerability. In a higher sense, responsibility seems inseparable from human existence, for man's humanity has a deep relationship to man's community and the human community is essentially dependent upon human answerability. This human capacity to be accountable may be fulfilled in response to a ruler or to the dictations of a powerful state or to the inner law of the "ought" or to the divine imperative of love.

Responsibility for different kinds of societies—the response of the primitive man to his rigid social structure and customs, the response of the modern man to a dictator, the response of a free man to his democratic community—has a significant variation in quality. A free society requires a large degree of responsiveness on the part of its citizens, from whom its direction comes. And for that reason responsibility in a democratic society, now in an age of transition, is complicated.

Education in democracy must be concerned with developing in man a quality of responsibility characterized by a personal inner control: self-rule; the fulfillment of the spirit of the law and not the letter only; a holding of oneself accountable to others beyond the requirements of law. A closer examination of this notion of responsibility, however, soon involves the most difficult concepts of freedom, personality, and community, and it becomes evident that the problem of responsibility in a free society in transition is a significant challenge in contemporary education.

The depth of the meaning of responsibility is illustrated in a negative sense by increasing evidences in modern society of irresponsible relationships among men. Pernicious trends toward impersonality have come about through the growth of great cities, wars, mass population shifts, radical changes in the traditional community, the mechanization of daily living, the weakening of family ties, and the questionable procedures of great corporations and bureaucracies. And only too often in the more direct and intimate personal relationships in the community there are increasing evidences of disunity in teacher-pupil relationships, in family relationships, business partnerships, neighborhood activities, and social circles; and there are the continuing divergences between rich and poor, manager and laborer, educated and uneducated, white man and black man, Occidental and Oriental, ad infinitum. Irresponsibility is highlighted in divorce, crime, political corruption, juvenile delinquency, parental apathy, and overresponsiveness to economic expediencies.

These tragic realities in our society point up more clearly the moral nature of education's task in helping to rebuild a disjointed world. Any educational system alive to the needs of this generation can hardly escape the obligation to renew the intangible, cohesive, constructive ingredients of human personality by which men can live in free community. If responsibility is not supported in a democratic society, the alternative is the ascendancy of a different kind of social order which insures compliance through the use of force and fear. Thus responsibility becomes a focal point for any education fulfilling a constructive role in a society vitally concerned with a free way of life.

The task of developing responsible persons is presented, therefore, as one of the basic problems of twentieth century education in America. The more intensively the problem is examined, the more profoundly it relates to the deep questions about the nature of man and his destiny. It soon becomes evident that there are philosophies of education which differ widely in their ideas about the nature of man and about the basis of human responsibility and about the means

to be used in developing responsible persons. These fundamental cleavages bear untoward consequences in educational
practice, showing over and over again the dangers of an
educational house divided against itself. That men will
always have their honest differences is not here a primary
concern; rather it is the evidences of continuing schisms at
the base which make the surface conflicts in education
doubly dangerous. So long as men of varying opinions can
stand upon a common foundation, they may remain relatively unperturbed by surface tensions; in such a case the
generous sharing of many divergent views ought to enhance
rather than impede education in a democracy. But when
the differences of view involve fundamental presuppositions,
we have reason to be seriously disturbed.

The primary task of this study is to compare and to contrast some of the outstanding contradictory world views in
American education today and to examine how these competitive views face the critical problem of developing responsible persons within the complex and disconcerting influences of the times. This comparative study bases itself
upon at least two important presuppositions: First, each of
the contrasting world views is considered actually a *faith*
insofar as it has something to say about education's task of
improving the community. As the Catholic and the communist imply, all education must ultimately be religious,
that is to say, based upon some kind of assumption about
the nature and destiny of man which is a moving faith.

Furthermore, a consideration of one educational philosophy as secular and another as religious weakens the basis
for comparison. Nor is this secular-religious dualism either
necessary or desired. John Dewey the progressive, Theodore
Brameld the radical, and T. S. Eliot the conservative, for
example, discover themselves in general agreement with the
argument that the secular versus the religious is a dualism
of dualisms which ought to be got rid of as quickly as pos-

sible. Thus it becomes possible to speak of Dewey's "common faith" based upon the scientific method, of Brameld's radical faith based upon the expansive powers of the common man, of Robert Hutchins' faith in the divine spark of reason which distinguishes man from the animal, and of the Christian faith in God, "a Spirit, infinite, and eternal."

Second, it is proposed that the educational philosophies under consideration can best be understood and evaluated in terms of their basic concepts of the nature of man. At this fundamental level one may understand more clearly the "whys" of practice and gain significant insights into the reasons for conflicts in practice. In the concept of man's nature lies the heart of faith and practice. To become interested in the aims of education is to ask what education is for. If it is agreed that education is for the improvement of man, one is immediately involved in metaphysical and theological problems: What is the nature of man and what is man for?

Having briefly outlined the nature of the problem of responsibility in education and suggested a framework for its further consideration, I will undertake in the following chapters a fuller investigation of what is understood to be the basis of human responsibility, the soil in which it best flourishes, and the means of cultivating it. I assume that all persons should possess in their souls a deep sense of obligation and responsibility in their relationships to their neighbors. The real problem is: How are such responsible persons to be developed within the twentieth century setting with its disconcerting scientific and technological trends and its unsettling social, political, economic, and religious aberrations?

PART ONE

Progressivism

CHAPTER ONE

Progressivism in Outline

IN THE long and tortuous transition from medieval to modern civilization in Western history the changing concept of authority was basic and crucial. In medieval times the Christian church was the authority which permeated all levels of society. By contrast the modern mind is far removed generally from that medieval faith. Currently a wide range of contradictory authorities has supplanted the church and its sovereign God. Pragmatism today is one of the faiths in revolt against older traditions.

Pragmatism the theory, which is progressivism in practice insofar as education is concerned, is a philosophy peculiarly American, a philosophy which appeals to the common man of action because it counts experience as the real basis for knowing. Three quite uncommon American philosophers—Charles Peirce, William James, and John Dewey—supplied in the main the intellectual impetus which forged this doctrine in its American form out of the revolutionary scientific and philosophical developments of the nineteenth century. Peirce gave the pragmatic ideal philosophical stature by emphasizing that the truth of an idea is to be formulated in terms of the sum of its practical consequences and that the practical consequences mark the limit of truth. William James, one of the most influential of American thinkers and an intimate of Charles Peirce, popularized the pragmatic idea of Peirce and added radical interpretations with which Peirce vigorously disagreed. These new concepts of James will be discussed in some detail in the next chapter.

William James' outline of a universe which was open

and novel, free from medieval universals and modern Kantian categories, evolved into a Jamesian concept of relative truth based on experience. This concept provided a springboard for John Dewey, who became in the twentieth century a revolutionary figure in education zealously proclaiming the thesis that the learner learns by doing.

Possibly the briefest and most efficient approach to an understanding of the present day implications of pragmatism in education is the attempt to understand the pragmatic view of the nature of truth. Philosophies throughout the ages, observed John Dewey, have been burdened with the quest for the transcendental truth, conceived as certainty, absoluteness, abiding, immutable, the same yesterday, today, and forever.[1] This historical concept of truth had a natural kind of evolution, according to Dewey. Men have always feared uncertainty and thus have fabricated the much needed verities in which they found consolation and spiritual protection in times of stress and danger. This longing for certitude is traceable through the folklores of primitive peoples. As they relived their experiences around the campfires, savages filled their tales with dramatic incidents, using poetic license to make their stories more tellable. In this way they developed myth, tradition, and religion.

To the extent that folklore remained in practical relationship with activity it retained an empirical factual content; to the extent that it related to the realm of drama and imagination it tended to become mythical and religious. These tendencies accounted for the emergence of two spheres of tradition: the religious and the practical, each more or less separated from the other. This emergence of the religious and the practical provided the early foundations for the continuing dualisms of history: the traditional polar positions of thought and action, theory and practice, mind

1 Much of the material in this chapter is based upon four of John Dewey's books: *The Quest for Certainty; Reconstruction in Philosophy; Democracy and Education;* and *Logic: The Theory of Inquiry.*

and matter, the spirit and the flesh, the philosopher and the artisan. The realm of thought directly related to physical activity was considered the baser realm. On the other hand the realm of pure thought was conveniently separated from the world of practical activity; this realm was rationalized into a lofty position by man's quest for what was unchanging and eternal. The further the idea was removed from practice, the more an aura of certainty it attained.

Whereas the primitives posited their certainties in myths and simple religions, wrote Dewey, the later philosophers transformed the primitive religions and myths into the kingdom of metaphysics, supplanting superstition with reason. Later, quite profound theologies came into existence, combining faith with reason and giving extended support to a belief in the supernatural. It was against this theological and philosophical version of truth that pragmatism revolted.

The substance of this revolt first of all is the denial that we can demonstrate the reality of absolutes, theological, philosophical, or otherwise. Man can only know through experience the interaction between an individual and his environment. Since the relationship between the individual and his environment is continually changing, there can be no absolute knowledge. Meaningful knowledge has to do with the relationships of objects and individuals considered as organic objects. The traditional concern about the thing in itself and all of the other intangible so-called realities about which the theological and philosophical experts have never been able to agree is considered unnecessary, confusing, obsolete, and untenable.

Knowledge is obtained and conclusions are made in terms of experience. These conclusions are then subjected to further tests of experience to determine their continuing validity. In other words, experiences are evaluated in terms of consequences. Truth is not a fixed rule by which to measure experience, but something continually discovered in the consequences of experience. Truth is in the future, not in the past. Truth is relative, not absolute and eternal.

According to the pragmatist, laws are not statements of absolutes but predictions of probability. Nature is not immutable. We learn nature's ways through experience, and this relative knowledge is subjected to further testings in experience. Contemplation of "what" in terms of the "thing in itself" is labeled a spurious enterprise.

What are the practical outcomes of this Deweyan pragmatic revolt against traditional authorities? Simply that all so-called absolute truths and dogmatisms which confuse and antagonize people are removed from the scene of learning; intolerance and fanaticism are likewise dissipated. Philosophy comes down to earth and assumes a practical role: the tremendously challenging task of working out the scientific method in ever increasing higher levels of discovery and control of the forces of nature—the discovery of truth which works.

As far as the pragmatist can tell, there is no unchanging reality above this natural, dynamic universe. Man's hope is to adjust to this moving world as he knows it. He who resists is doomed; the plastic organisms survive. Nature deals harshly with the individual who has lost his ability to adjust and to turn with the blows. Man ought to understand that he is a part of the natural flux, not a being who lives above it; his nature is continuous with the nature which produced him. Man ought not, however, to be considered a passive organism in the face of his environment. In fact all living organisms not only adapt to the environment, but they also do something to the environment in return. Even a clam does something to its environment. The savage does much more, but he transforms his environment much less than the civilized man who has intelligently discovered ways to control the environment. Human intelligence is a natural capacity by which man can anticipate a favorable outcome and can order his means accordingly, thus making a thousandfold more effective the process of favorably transforming the environment. And this is the glory of man in his present civilized estate.

So it seems evident that pragmatism is an optimistic philosophy. Man's world of experience constitutes his only world, and a unique human organism has evolved an intelligence which can control this world of experience. In other words, progress is possible. The gospel of progress is the wellspring of hope and determination. Change is inevitable, but there is no reason why change cannot be controlled for the better by means of human intelligence. Pragmatism is above all "the belief in man's ability to face the world with his own skills and powers and to solve his problems through his own active intelligence."[2] Men who are intelligent and able to direct their environments need no longer consign themselves to determining so-called eternal verities. Intelligent men put their faith in a control of the natural experienced world, not in the dictates of some faraway spiritual world.

Given, in education, the philosophy that thinking and learning are the human organism in interaction with the natural environment and that human intelligence is a product of this interaction, one has a graphic outline for revolutionary developments in the traditional schoolroom. Activity becomes the theme. The pupil learns by doing.

In the light of pragmatic doctrines the older traditional formal educational procedures stand in judgment. Older doctrines are considered sterile because they deny meaningful activity. Pragmatically, education is valid and effective to the extent that it involves the enriching dynamic interaction of the organism with its environment. According to John Dewey, educational activity should be essentially free, expanding, moving, stimulating. Life is growth, and educa-

2 Theodore Brameld, *Patterns of Educational Philosophy: A Democratic Interpretation* (Yonkers-on-Hudson, N. Y., 1950), 97.

tion is the assistance of growth: vigorous, responsive, forward looking, unhampered. Life is development and development is life. Education for the child is "living." The
educational activity is its own end. There need not be, in
education, preordained ends, but simply growth, the reconstruction of experience in terms of new experience. Education aims at continuous reconstruction of experience as
contrasted with preparation for a remote future or a formal
recapitulation of the past.

Education does not have set aims according to these views.
The object of education is continuing successful activity in
order that the individual may achieve the art of adjustment
to and control of his environment. Temporary ends are
primarily stimuli to action; when they are reached they
become steppingstones for further temporary ends. The
suspense which is engendered by the immediate temporary
goal substitutes for formal discipline. The pragmatic discipline does not artificially restrain the learner but confronts
him with the stimulating call of "interest."[3]

One final summary observation ought to be made before
proceeding to a more detailed and careful examination of
the pragmatic doctrine of the nature of man. Throughout
the works of John Dewey and some of his illustrious disciples
there is the recurring theme of education and democracy.
For the progressive, education is indeed the hope of democracy. Education through activity makes possible an enrich-
ment for all kinds of persons, the rich, the poor, the elite,
the worker. The collective strength of all the citizens constitutes a vigorous democracy. Enriching interaction re-
moves artificial barriers between all classes. Increased socialization between races, classes, and colors is the lifeblood
of a strong democracy. Interactivity involving all kinds of
children from all kinds of groups and levels in the public

3 This and the preceding paragraph outline one of the outstanding theses
of John Dewey's *Democracy and Education.*

school is the best possible insurance for an enlightened and vigorous democratic way of life. Pragmatism is progressivism's faith. Democracy is its faith in action, whether in the schoolroom or in the community.

CHAPTER TWO

A Pragmatic Concept of
the Nature of Man

IN THE best pragmatic tradition men are not sons of God but sons of earth. Man is a child of nature and is continuous with nature; nature is his origin, his home.

In philosophy naturalism, the basis for a pragmatic interpretation of man's constitution, is not the naive or literary admiration of nature as opposed to the artificialities of civilization, but the metaphysical basis for explaining the origin and destiny of man. Naturalistic philosophy assumes that "the universe requires no supernatural cause or government, but is self-existent, self-explanatory, self-operating, and self-directing."[1] The idea of a self-sufficient universe seems dominant today in the sciences—particularly biology, psychology, and sociology—considered basic these days to the formulation of educational theory. Darwinian evolution, the doctrine of progress within the natural continuum, and the hypothesis that eventually all phenomena may be explained in naturalistic terms all imply that higher human nature too is subject to a natural and evolutionary explanation. Sidney Hook, an educational experimentalist, contends that there is really no genuine evidence which supports the idea that man may claim a nature qualitatively distinct from the natural environment which supports him. Man, insisted Ingersoll, is part and parcel of nature. "Nature 'produces man without purpose and obliterates him without regret.'

1 B. A. G. Fuller, in Dagobert Runes (ed.), *The Dictionary of Philosophy* (New York, 1942), 205.

. . . Man is the highest intelligence."[2] Revolutionary assumptions such as these about man and his nature have given fresh vigor to philosophical views dedicated to the eventual emancipation of man from the stubborn grasp of traditional, supernatural, and rational concepts of his nature which are believed to have impeded immeasurably the progress of the human race.

Against the naturalistic world picture the traditional convictions about man are labeled incompatible, out of order, out of date. A synthesis of the old and the new seems unattainable. Any suggestion of a supernatural element necessary to man's progress destroys the evolutionary framework of the naturalistic faith which postulates the orderly step-by-step progression of nature from the simple to the more complex. Possibly the most challenging task of the naturalist is to explain the complexity of the evolutionary process which connects man's higher moral and intellectual nature with his physical nature so that finally human progress may be charted to include man's spiritual capacities as well as his physical capacities.

To explain "naturally" the complex nature of the human being necessitates a radical revision of the traditional concepts of man's higher faculties: his intelligence, mind, will, esthetic appreciations, moral capacities—all of which distinguish him so notably from the lower creatures. The task of the naturalist is to dignify the natural process and to make it consonant with the loftiest of human expressions, to show that supposed transcendent characteristics in man are after all the fulfillments of nature operating at its higher levels. It must be shown that man is not a citizen of two worlds; he is a creature of one world—this world. He is not a dualism of mind and body, but a single creation of the natural world. It must be demonstrated that in the final

2 Ralph H. Gabriel, *The Course of American Democratic Thought* (New York, 1940), 180.

analysis the "mind" is not a spiritual entity, but a natural functional expression of the whole organism, however complex it may be.

For the progressivist, man's mind, like his body, is continuous with nature. Progressivism is much indebted to William James, who finally effected at least a philosophical emancipation from the traditional concept of man's mind as a spiritual entity. Preceding James, a long line of eminent Western philosophers had seriously concerned themselves with epistemological problems, the problems of *how we know*. In the nineteenth century, with a kind of snowballing accumulation of scientific evidence bolstering the naturalistic interpretation of man and his universe, the pace of philosophical speculation also quickened. Auguste Comte and Herbert Spencer particularly committed themselves to the philosophical assignment of naturalizing the mind, making it continuous with the natural process in order that mind the spiritual entity should no longer pose itself as a barrier to a thoroughgoing scientific understanding of the nature of man.

An essay written by William James toward the end of his career, entitled "Does Consciousness Exist?"[3] may be considered a climactic philosophical treatise serving finally to remove the traditional mind-body dualism which had grievously perplexed the earlier philosophers. William James in his essay concluded, in summary, that thoughts are made of the same stuff things are.

In the first place William James argued that the mind is not a kind of intangible driver which sits on the mental platform of the brain and directs the movements of the body. The mind is really not an entity at all, but a function or quality of interaction involving the organism and the environment. Herein can be noted the shift of interest from

3 William James, *Essays on Radical Empiricism* (New York, 1922).

"product" to "process." Mind is a process, not a substance. But how can this be?

The new interpretation of human consciousness can be understood "if we start with the supposition that there is only one primal stuff or material in the world, a stuff of which everything is composed, and if we call that stuff 'pure experience' then knowing can easily be explained as a particular sort of relation. . . . The relation itself is a part of pure experience; one of its 'terms' becomes the subject . . . the knower, the other becomes the object known."[4]

This basic "stuff," whatever it is, which constitutes the universe is involved in an endless variety of relationships. The relationships themselves constitute experiences. All objects (dogs, chairs, water) are stuffs of experience in unique relationships, and these relationships constitute the experience of dogs, chairs, water.

Possibly this idea can be somewhat more simply described with the use of an elementary example from the field of chemistry, an illustration which James did not himself use but which seems to follow from his technical treatise on the subject of consciousness. Suppose the substance "water" is considered as an example of the significance of relationships and how these relationships are themselves experiences. Hydrogen is one of the stuffs of experience, and likewise oxygen. When in nature these two stuffs come into peculiar relationship the result is a new stuff of experience called water.

With this illustration in mind let us turn to James' explanation of the nature of consciousness. The example of hydrogen and oxygen in a peculiar relationship resulting in the experience of water points up in a elemental way, perhaps, the significance of the relationship of the human organism to the environment resulting in a new experience called consciousness. As the hydrogen in relation to the

4 James, 4.

oxygen produces a new quality of experience called water, so the organism in relation to the environment results in a new quality of experience called consciousness. To carry the analogy a step further: When the relationship between hydrogen and oxygen is broken, the experience of water vanishes. When the relationship between the organism and the environment is broken, the mind vanishes. Organismic-environmental interaction equals mind or consciousness. On the other hand, no interaction—no mind. Possibly this illustration points out in a dim sense, for after all it is the mysterious fact of consciousness which is here being dealt with, the implications of "externalization" of the mind in the Jamesian sense. The mind is no more "inside" the body than water is inside either the hydrogen or the oxygen. Water is the *product* of the hydrogen-oxygen relationship. Consciousness is the product of organism in relationship to environment. Consciousness or "mind" is not to be discovered through abstraction but by addition.

In one respect, at least, the illustration of water as an example of relationship does not satisfactorily represent the quality of consciousness in the sense that consciousness is actually an activity and not a product. Possibly the simple example of oxygen combining with carbon which results in "burning" would more accurately accent the concept of mind as a process of "thinking."

The reduction of all reality to experience strikes out of the philosophical agenda some of the dualisms which have plagued the intelligentsia of previous centuries. If all reality is experience, the philosopher can bypass such problems as the physical and the spiritual, thought and action (or more specifically, mind and matter). It is in reference to the critical problem of mind and matter that William James comes to the conclusion that thoughts are made of the same stuff things are.

Consider the illustration which James uses in showing

how this dilemma has been eliminated in the new concept of mind. One may suppose himself looking at a book. Actually there seem to be two books involved. First, there is the book on the table, and second, there is the same book in the mind. The problem: Are there really two books or only one book? If there is one book, which is the real book, the copy on the table or the copy in the mind? James insists that there is only one book, or rather only one experience of a book. Keeping in mind the previously illustrated idea of what is consciousness, namely the organism in relation with the environment, one could assume in this case that the human organism is one stuff of experience interacting with a particular set of relationships in the environment (the book) resulting in consciousness of a book, which is a new experience. Consciousness of a book is an experience, a single unified phenomenon, which has two aspects: the thought of book in the objective sense and the book thought of in the subjective sense. The "book" is neither a material substance nor a copy of a material substance in the mind, but the "book" is an *experience,* one experience, one book, having its objective and subjective sides of the coin of "experience."

In this way William James reduced all realities not to mind, not to matter, but experience. Consciousness is not mind in the traditional sense, but a phenomenon of relationships, and relationships are experience. Since relationships exist "between" objects and have no inner reality, consciousness understood as a relationship is external. This is William James' philosophical externalization of the mind. If the mind therefore is not an inner reality, it need not be considered as a further obstacle to the naturalization of the human individual. The complete removal of the human mind as a spiritual entity clears the way for a consistent evolutionary naturalistic formulation of the nature of man's higher capacities and moral proclivities.

The biological organism of man is understood as an extremely complex and sensitive mechanism, itself the product of a natural evolutionary process. The emergence of the "mind" late in the evolutionary series signifies nature in a new dimension, possibly involving new and higher laws becoming aware of ends and values. The continuing scientific investigations of the higher capacities of the human organism accent two significant aspects of human life even in its most primitive forms, namely, the bent toward association and the invention of language, which provide the basis for the development of the "human" out of the man.

George Mead, one of the lesser known but important pragmatic philosophers, outlined in detail how it happened that man became self-conscious and human.[5] Man in his subhuman existence learned to live in groups. One of the requirements of group living was some form of communication, which is even now in evidence among many animal groups. Man, possessing an unusually highly developed nervous system, eventually became aware of the possibilities of utilizing natural signs and gestures. He realized after a long time that the choice of a certain sign could evoke from his associates a preferred response. A growing preoccupation with the relationships between lingual stimulus and response provided the basis for man's eventual arrival at self-consciousness. In other words, the evolution of the use of language and the evolution of human self-consciousness exemplify a basic interrelationship.

The meaningful conscious communication by bodily gestures was a cumulative affair which resulted finally in a vocal-cord refinement of gestures known as language. "Language is thus the bridge between the unconscious course of things in 'nature' and the self-conscious life of man."[6] And this concept coincides with George Mead's ideas about the social

[5] George Mead, *Mind, Self, and Society* (Chicago, 1934), Part II.
[6] John L. Childs, *Education and Morals* (New York, 1950), 71.

basis for the development of consciousness and mind in the human organism. The substitution of symbols for the more or less cumbersome acts was indescribably significant, giving the human animal a new leverage on his environment and new relationships with fellow creatures which made possible the formation of what is now called human culture. Man is born into the present cultural environment as an animal organism. The culture which surrounds him, itself a natural evolutionary formation, transforms the animal baby into the human person. Man is not human in his own right but by virtue of his relationship to his cultural environment. "Selfhood is . . . a self-other product."[7] Men are all members one of another. Selfhood is formed in terms of "otherhood" relationships.

A far-reaching and all important conclusion follows from this understanding of the nature of man: Human nature is plastic and mutable, subject to change. The human organism, being the product of aeons of interaction with its natural environment, has reached the present high estate progressively, and scientific evidence indicates that this progression should continue. There is no scientific basis for assuming that human nature cannot change.

With man the prospect of change is an exciting outlook because the emergence of a new factor "intelligence" means that nature can be controlled and changes for the better can be stepped up a thousandfold. Think of the breathtaking implications for modern man who has within his grasp the means of self-creation, literally self-promoting and self-directing his progress toward ever higher levels of knowing and being.

Basically the crowning glory of the self-realizing pragmatic person is his *intelligence,* by means of which moral progress is possible as well as the progressive control of the physical environment. Man's intelligence, too, is a completely natural

[7] William Heard Kilpatrick, *Philosophy of Education* (New York, 1951), 40.

phenomenon supplanting the older concept of reason—that supposed immaterial faculty which qualitatively distinguishes him from animals. Intelligence is ability developed through organismic-environmental interaction, just as the human organism itself from the beginning developed through interaction with the natural environment. With the development of language, experience became symbols, and symbols made possible a shorthand high-speed projection of causes and effects, which is thinking.

Thinking in a truly reflective sense does not occur until the organism is blocked by some kind of obstacle in the path of desire. Removing the obstacle through the process of reflection results in the formulation of a hypothesis. Testing this hypothesis by experience is commonly called problem solving. When intelligence is increased in depth as a result of broad, enriching, successful encounters of organism with environment, the individual gains extra leverage and control over the environment for future encounters. Intelligence is knowing through experience, and "knowing marks the conversion of the undirected changes into changes directed toward an intended conclusion."[8] This naturally evolved human consciousness is the finest attribute of man in contrast with the lower animal organisms. Intelligence is nature distinguishing itself at the highest levels.

In conclusion it should be noted that this pragmatic concept of man is primarily individualistic. There are no universal laws; there is no universal being. The universe is pluralistic, and each individual in this kind of universe works out the quality of his own existence in his relations with the environment.

Pragmatism in its understanding of man does not dissociate itself from the individualizing trend begun by the Renaissance and the Reformation. The Reformation insistence upon the infinite worth of the individual soul and

8 John Dewey, *The Quest for Certainty* (New York, 1929), 205.

the right of every man to be his own priest in the working out of his own salvation is clearly a part of the pragmatic ideal. The pragmatic man fundamentally is a superprotestant, who not only protests against ecclesiasticism but against all authorities, religious or secular. This characteristic individualism in pragmatism will later be emphasized as a distinguishing feature in a contrast between the pragmatic and the social reconstructionist concepts of man's nature.

CHAPTER THREE

A Progressive Solution to the Problem of Developing Responsibility

THE DEVELOPMENT of responsibility is without question a basic and serious problem for the pragmatist. The morale of youth in the face of twentieth century social and moral schism presents a disturbing picture. The democratic ideal in action is shaken to the foundations because of a tendency of the youth in America to be more taken up with the rights of freedom than with its obligations. A recent survey of more than 2,000 high school students discovered that "over two-thirds [of the students] defined democracy solely in terms of rights and liberties without reference to responsibilities."[1] It hardly seems possible that the situation should be otherwise, since our whole society is confused and erratic, and the conduct of elders and leaders often irresponsible. Even so, a democracy cannot long endure if the youth which is its hope does not learn effectively its lessons of responsibility. Democracy, which is a majority way of life, cannot hope to function successfully if the majority is not composed of responsible self-governing persons.

For the pragmatist the moral problem must find its solution within the natural continuum, since the validities of divine absolutes and rational postulates are denied. Roughly speaking, it may be anticipated that the progressivist and the educational reconstructionist will deal with the problem of responsibility in terms of organismic-environmental relationships within the natural flux defined as "experience."

---

[1] Educational Policies Commission, *Learning the Ways of Democracy* (Washington, 1940), 47.

The classical humanist by contrast will attack the problem in terms of a human nature distinct from and above the natural flux, while the Christian viewpoint will be taken up primarily with the existence of God, infinite and eternal, as the ground for responsible relationships between man.

With the progressivist, man by nature is not depraved or deprived, not good or bad actually, but a morally neutral dynamic organism possessing drives and energies which are neither wholesome nor unwholesome. The growing organism's basic need is direction and refinement, and this is the task of the surrounding culture which humanizes him. Man's conscience, as it develops, is not the echo of a divine command but the integration of the customs of the culture. Man in his biological and spiritual development is continuous with the rest of nature. The twin oracles of psychology and sociology, overflowing with scientific evidence relating to every facet of man's nature and activity, provide a considerably enlarged basis for the theory of a natural morality.

Although the pragmatic solution to the problem of responsibility appears to be modern, its primary theme is evident in the influential writings of Jean Jacques Rousseau, Charles Darwin, and Herbert Spencer, each in turn being indebted to some extent to David Hume. During the period when these men were making a significant contribution to the new ethics, there was a parallel trend toward disintegration of older ethical foundations. Possibly a few references should be made first to the negativistic trend: the revolt against traditional ethical supports.

Particularly during the last half of the nineteenth century in America there was a significant turning away from theological faith as the basis of moral conduct. Morality was more and more divorced from theology, especially in its puritanical expressions. Many intellectual leaders assumed that theology was more to be associated with moral confusion than with moral virtue in society; that religions which propagated the concept of sin were perverting the wholesomeness of personality, distorting men's souls, dissipating their vitalities; that a devotion to fixed ends demonstrated a timidity to face the world; that persons theologically oriented simply wanted a guarantee of success in advance of action. Fixed principles were condemned as a refuge for the timid.

During this critical half of the nineteenth century many intellectuals revolted against the idea of an autocratic God holding over the heads of men the threat of hell and the incentive of heaven in order to promote moral conduct. There was the accusation that the Christian religion claimed men's loyalties for another world, thus attenuating their zeal and energies to solve the immediate problems at hand in this world; that this kind of doctrine led naive people to a faith in false values, beclouding the challenge toward the good life here and now. In addition, men advanced the argument that the traditional emphasis upon theological doctrine fomented religious wars and built up great walls of separation between peoples. Too, the naive superstitions of the simple were taken advantage of, in the name of religion, by unscrupulous vested interests. In this revolt of the intelligentsia, serious effort was made to eliminate as efficiently as possible that which was considered opiate, that which neutralized the vitalities of men in action.

This attack on traditional Christian faith was paralleled with an energetic dedication to the task of substituting an experimental scientific basis for conduct, adaptable and adjustable to the changing social patterns. This new morality, as would be expected, was related to the concept of a naturalized man completely capable of ordering his life and society without extranatural assistance. This new office to which man elected himself, that of fulfilling his own destiny with the power of his own science, was in itself a new con-

cept of human responsibility quite different from the timid
disposal of the fate of men at the hands of the Almighty.

It should be mentioned at this point that the truly difficult
feature of a naturalistic ethics is a scientifically and philosophically plausible development of that sense of "ought"
within the natural continuum, especially in the face of scientific insistence that the natural continuum is a mechanistic
system of cause and effect. Yet nineteenth century thinkers
such as Auguste Comte, Charles Darwin, Thomas Huxley,
and Herbert Spencer worked out a scientific evolutionary
scheme which has been generally acceptable to many contemporary philosophers.

The naturalistic seeds of moral responsibility are to be
discovered in Darwinian and Spencerian descriptions of
"sympathy" as a common characteristic of higher animals,
underlying the progression toward a social or herd life. In
the element of sympathy is seen the evolutionary germ of a
human moral conscience. Love and sympathy are instinctive feelings already evident in social animals. Morally good
actions are motivated by instinctive social feelings, and these
social feelings evolve to higher levels through the process
of natural selection. In the experience of the race there has
developed an awareness of the fact that long range results
are more to be sought after than immediate gratification of
desire. This, specifically, is the basis of responsible action.
The dispositions toward responsibility are evolved from the
culture, which is itself unaffected by any supposed supernatural influence.

With Rousseau the same theme is enlarged upon. Natural
pity is the forerunner of those humane characteristics which
supply the basis for responsible conduct such as generosity,
benevolence, and friendship. Naturalism discovers the possibility of developing a "new evangel" which in terms of
sympathetic emotions finally expresses itself as love. The
evolutionary process produces a kind of charity in action

not supported by any kind of divine influence but simply founded upon the scientific gospel of man the son of nature and evolution.

This scientific approach was subscribed to by John Dewey in his early years, and later he seemed more convinced than ever that moral values arise in organic evolution, that natural-born intelligence is the key to the formulation of these values. This Deweyan juxtaposition of intelligence and morality is a significant sign of things to come—a pragmatic clue to the problem of how to develop responsible persons.

There are at least four important planks in the pragmatic platform which support a twentieth century progressive program for developing responsibility in the learner. The first is the assumption that satisfaction is the final goal of the human organism. Whereas some of the older traditions emphasized happiness as a kind of satisfaction derived through the exercise of reason, the pragmatist follows the lead of the Epicurean and the utilitarian who emphasize the hedonistic idea of pleasure as the end. Whereas some of the philosophers like Kant emphasized duty rationally understood, the pragmatist considers man a goal-seeking animal, and in this sense sensual satisfaction seems necessarily the only scientifically understandable end for man, particularly since the whole significance of man's existence is to be found within the natural continuum. It is nothing less than a utilitarian assumption that basically all conduct is determined by the expectation of pleasure and the avoidance of pain. In the final analysis satisfaction must be the basis of ethical formulations. There is no absolute moral code, and the problem of morals must essentially be a matter of taste.

All organisms are goal-seeking. The natural bent toward satisfaction of desires is normal and good. The moral problem arises when there is a conflict between goals. The strong impulses of the organism toward gratification of wants are intense natural drives toward the fulfillment of what seems important, what gives the greatest satisfaction. Man, however, is not to capitulate to a crude kind of satisfaction, thus inviting dire consequences. Nature has provided a way of escape from a gross hedonism in the development of human intelligence. By intelligence it is possible for a man to evaluate consequences and to choose the long term rather than the short term satisfaction.

The relationship between satisfaction and the development of responsibility is more direct than might be supposed, according to the pragmatic interpretation. To phrase it in the graphic terms of William Clayton Bower, it is when you get the "feel" of a value that it grips you, and you are motivated by your desire (autonomous motivation) to close the gap between that which is and that which ought to be.[2] Laurence Sears, in accord with the pragmatic tradition of experimentation, has actually made empirical studies of the relationship between satisfaction and responsibility. Sears came to the conclusion, based upon a number of case studies, that persons tend to develop responsibility in higher levels of conduct when they discover *satisfaction* accruing from it. Satisfaction derived from intelligent activity is a spur toward responsible activity. Actually, intelligent activity is responsible activity, and the satisfaction derived from it develops the habit of responsibility. The final test is living—whether it is more satisfactory. The more satisfactory life as a consequence of action is the guide for further responsible activity.

A second basic theme which is central in the pragmatic solution to the problem of developing responsibility is the concept of experience—the conscious interaction of the organism with its environment. Experience is interaction, and interaction is synonymous with activity. Activity in the progressive sense is the foundation of the good life. Indeed, "the kingdom of God cometh not with observation."[3] Moral virtue comes not from divine authority, or laws rationally

2 William Clayton Bower in a class discussion at the University of Kentucky, Summer, 1951.
3 Luke 17:20.

supported, or law enforcement based upon enlightened self-interest, or deification of state, but from social interaction, meaningful activity, experience. The problem of responsibility centers not in the person or in law, but in the environment, or more technically, in organismic-environmental interactions. The significant task involved is environmental conversion rather than personal conversion.

The long history of the evolution of an individual is a story about the interaction of organism with environment, and the history of the development of moral responsibility is logically a continuation of the same process. If the continuing evolution of man demonstrates anything at all, it points up the fact that even genuine knowledge and fruitful understanding have their origin in experience, interaction, doing. "If, as Mead has pointed out, the self is a social product, and, as Henry Churchill King once suggested, the richness and quality of one's life consists of the number of relations one discerns and fulfills, the interaction of the growing person with his social world is a most fertile source of moral and spiritual values."[4]

When learning from life situations becomes the basis of education, it becomes inquiry, investigation, and choosing between available courses of action. This kind of education with its ever present emphasis upon the element of decision—choices between options and their relationships to consequences—involves the essence of responsible activity.

John Dewey contends with remarkable consistency that one cannot divorce the good or bad person from the environment. The development of the good persons depends upon a good environment. As the flower seed in the desert cannot fulfill its destiny except someone change its arid environment, so the human individual cannot fulfill his moral capacities except his environment is modified accordingly. A miracle is not necessary to grow a flower in the desert or

4 William Clayton Bower, *Moral and Spiritual Values in Education* (Lexington, 1952), 51.

to develop an individual who is morally responsible, but both require, primarily, the intelligent reconstruction of the environment.

The concept of the "good" itself is the product of experience, and being experientially derived, it is relative, varying with the situation. Rather than a unified law of the "good" there are "goods" or values, and these values reside in experience. They do not inhere in an external or supernal authority but grow out of experience and re-enter experience.

This dominant emphasis on experience constitutes the theoretical framework of the widely publicized "Kentucky Movement" fathered philosophically by William Clayton Bower, professor emeritus of The University of Chicago Theological School. This movement has clearly recognized the desperate need in public education for a means of developing values to substitute for the older value supports which have to some extent crumbled. In a sense there is in the public schools, according to the pragmatists, a kind of moral vacuum existing during this transition from the earlier age supported ethically by a divine authority and the coming age which requires a new kind of moral support more in harmony with the scientific spirit.

The Kentucky Movement, realistically appraising the breakdown of traditional moral supports, proceeds on the basis of a new assumption, namely, that value can be discovered in the routine experience of the school community. Values are potentially present in all experience. Where a situation is evaluated and decided upon, there values appear. These values are ethically significant, but they do not necessarily derive their significance from theological support. Rather they are discovered and validated intelligently, always subject to the test of experience. Any virtue can be validated only by trying it out intelligently. When a learner in activity faces an alternative choice, which is continually the case in an ideal pragmatic educational setting, he decides (ideally speaking) in terms of his fullest intelligence, and it is the decision in terms of intelligence which is the basis for the development of the responsible individual. Actually, any other understanding of the basis of morality is in itself immoral, since it fails to consider the individual as an end in himself possessing within himself the right of freedom of choice. An attempt at indoctrination, for example, disregards the freedom of choosing and eventually weakens the habit of "responsibly" making choices and responsibly acting in terms of those choices. The richer the program of educational activities, the more intelligent the learner becomes. The higher the intelligence, resulting from meaningful interactions with the environment, the more satisfactory the choices are. The more satisfactory these choices, the more moral they are. The greater the exercise in moral choices, as a result of an activity program in education, the more developed is the learner's habit of being responsible. Thus, through intelligence developed and reconstructed continually through activity which is meaningful interaction with the environment, it becomes possible for persons to learn more and more what "ought" to be. Intelligence becomes the dynamic support of responsible conduct. Intelligence is the "essence of virtue, as it is of responsibility."[5]

As was mentioned previously, John Dewey early in his writings identified morals with intelligence, classifying both as products of experience—interaction with the environment. Education conceived as guided experience is therefore basically moral activity, developing in the learner a natural kind of conscience holding him accountable to his society. Dewey's book *Reconstruction in Philosophy* is dedicated to the theme that intelligence realized as the scientific method has revolutionized man's physical world, and in like manner intelligence realized ethically should result in a moral revolution

[5] Laurence Sears, *Responsibility: Its Development Through Punishment and Reward* (New York, 1932), 191.

providing the outstanding scientific advancement in the twentieth century.

This progressive persuasion that values are resident in experience (that is to say, experience within the natural continuum) is the contemporary scientific basis for a new education fulfilling requirements for modern man in the new age. Youth nurtured in experimental methods will reject authoritarianism and supernaturalism in favor of the assumption that "to be moral you must be intelligent, and . . . in order to be intelligent you have to take critical account of actual alternatives."[6] Natural intelligence and the scientific method become the modern supplanters of the older ethical authorities. Natural intelligence operating in the field of experience takes on a religious aspect as choices between options involve choices between values. Things are not good or bad in themselves but as they are of value in satisfying the wants of individuals. When a want is discovered to have worth, it becomes a value. Each individual should choose between possible courses of action so as to promote the good life for all persons, and such choices are moral. The intelligent choice is made in terms of consequences, and to act in the light of an understanding of consequences fundamentally involves the principle of responsibility. The intelligent understanding of consequences is the best insurance for responsible action. This concept dignifies and deepens the meaning of responsibility as compared to the naive choice between alternatives based upon some authoritative decree.

Consequences cannot be separated from conditions. Judgments about values cannot be separated from judgments about facts. Intelligence and moral judgment are united in common embrace, committed to the development of the responsible individual. Growth in intelligence implies a concomitant growth in moral perspicuity.

[6] Childs, *Education and Morals,* 168-69.

A third feature of the pragmatic ideal intimately related to the problem of developing responsible persons is the progressivist explanation of the will, or more explicitly, the freedom of the will. This is an essential problem in the light of the pragmatic insistence that intelligent choices are basically important in the development of responsibility.

The human will in the modern sense is not understood as a special kind of entity which enables a person to decide on a certain course of action, but rather as an intelligent response to the particular alternative path which exerts the most "pull" on the person because it offers the best consequences. Hence the idea of the will as a "push" within the person is supplanted with an emphasis on the "pull" of the environment and the response of the organism to this pull. The moral exercise of the will is really an intellectually controlled response to one of several possible choices.

"Freedom" of the will appears at that point where intelligence assumes control. The pragmatic universe, open and dynamic, allows for an infinite variety of new relationships within the natural flux. Anything can happen. There are no universal laws or foreordained guiding principles or supernatural providences. As intelligence emerges in this kind of a world, it becomes possible to fore-evaluate the results of new relationships and new interactions in the environment. Intelligence with its prognosticating faculty can foresee; foreseeing, it controls and regulates interactions in favor of preferred consequences.

This is human freedom based upon human intelligence controlling the environment. Men acquire freedom from disease not by praying to an unseen power but through the intellectual control of the environment. Men acquire freedom from poverty and slavish conditions not by singing spirituals but through the intellectually guided revision of the environment, producing scientifically the methods and the machinery which dissipate these evils. Nature in her unregulated course tends to enslave man. Intelligence reverses the process and enslaves nature, making man free. Human intelligence is the foundation of human freedom. Freedom has its source in nature, or rather in intelligence, which is nature's highest purposive expression. "Our acts are *free* . . . because they are becoming *intelligent*. . . . We become free as we *learn* to *think*."[7]

The naive organism through natural desire seeks after satisfaction. The intelligent organism contemplates the consequences of its desired ends and *controls* the movement of the organism toward the fulfillment of its desires. The more complete the intellectual control, the greater are the dividends in human freedom. The greater the consciousness of human freedom, the greater the sense of responsibility for the choice of consequences. Intellectually man becomes aware of his free control of means toward new ends, and intellectually he realizes his responsibility for those ends. The exercise of intelligence naturally develops the habit of responsibility.

And finally there is the pragmatic ideal of fellowship which lies at the heart of the progressive solution to the problem of community, which is in turn inseparably related to the problem of responsibility: the relationship of the one to the many—the ideal relationship of the citizen to his neighbors.

For the pragmatist the narrow, unactive life is the sinful life. The interactive, responsive life is the good life. Given the element of "sympathy" in human nature which supports the bent toward community, it follows that the emphasis of a never ending variety of enriching interactive experiences exercising and intellectualizing the inherent "sympathy" in man should provide the natural basis for human fellowship. An active life involving all manner of contacts with all manner and conditions of men should deepen a man's sympa-

7 Childs, 151.

thetic understanding of his neighbor and his neighbor's views on life. A truly broadened understanding of other men through a life of activity and association with other men should prove a most effective and natural antidote to intolerance and human conflict. It is ignorance which separates men and causes them to act irresponsibly one toward another. By contrast, the self in continuous formation through its choices and interactions with persons and things becomes a wider and larger self, which implies the inclusion rather than the denial of enriching relationships.

The pragmatic concept of the democratic way of life provides the richest ground for the development of the ideal of fellowship. With democracy in action every person shares in the experiences, purposes, and responsibilities of the group. Group activity places a premium upon the interaction of persons as they are engaged in the accomplishment of a common goal. Every person in a democracy is a responsible sharer with others in the whole venture. An individual grows in personal responsibility as he realizes in a concrete manner the approval and the disapproval of the group in regard to his actions. Irresponsible action incurs group disapproval. Responsible action receives group approval. The sense of satisfaction which results from group approval develops the habit of acting responsibly. In this way the learner discovers through experience that his "deeds are imputed to him as their owner, not merely their creator. That he cannot disown them when the moment of their occurrence passes is the root of responsibility, moral as well as legal."[8]

As a final observation it seems practical to pose the question: How does this solution actually work in practice? What is a practical example of the pragmatic solution to the problem of developing responsibility actually taking place in the educative process?

[8] John Dewey, *Human Nature and Conduct* (New York, 1922), 117.

Possibly no more realistic and critical problem could be suggested than that of irresponsible race relationships which are notoriously evident in many segments of contemporary American society. What in this instance is the pragmatic solution? How are irresponsible relationships supplanted with the desired responsible associations between two unharmoniously related classes of individuals in a community, separated often by high walls of prejudice and misunderstanding?

Pragmatists believe that the school constitutes the medium in which the solution may best take place. Certainly the church as a social institution has seriously faltered in the face of this problem. In fact the church often is reactionary and impedes the progress toward better race relationships. Since, therefore, theological dicta are generally disqualified by the evidence of the poor works which flow from them, the pragmatist has a strong incentive to look elsewhere. And of course the "elsewhere" for the pragmatist is "experience." Proper experiences, as the basis, are the first requirement. The school provides a deliberate field of experiences which bear upon the problem. Since one cannot have experience without experiences, the actual guided interactions between races must take place within the school community. At least it is at this point that the start must be made. The multiplication of interracial experiences results in an expansion of intelligence which includes the intellectual appreciation of the other race. As children become more racially intelligent, they become more racially understanding—their sympathies are multiplied and refined. On the other hand, the multiplication of experiences and the expansion of intelligence for the so-called inferior group results in a freedom from ignorance which previously narrowed and enslaved them. The growth on their part in freer participation in the school community activity adds to the breadth of understanding and appreciation of all. Experience and intelligence are the basis of a genuine fellowship which can literally transcend the prejudicial ignorance-supported barriers of race. The foundation and the means to the solution of proper relationships between classes are actually to be found in the school environment where the young may grow naturally and wholesomely into attitudes of responsiveness toward, rather than divisiveness among, different kinds of peoples. Of course, pragmatically this is a hypothesis until it has been tested in actual experience. Yet, a widely developed intelligence suggests that this hypothesis is a good risk. Should the assumption prove valid in practice, the community will have moved one definite step forward in its moral venture, whereupon it proceeds to fulfill even greater responsibilities in the light of its reconstructed understanding of moral obligations.

In the final analysis it seems that the prime recurring emphasis of the pragmatist is the doctrine that the individual educated in a democratized and socialized environment is thereby enhanced with a natural intelligence which has the capacity of taking into account the consequences of acts, and this capacity provides the genuine basis of all responsible activity. To fulfill the pragmatic ideal of the intelligent person is to fulfill the progressivist concept of the responsible person.

PART TWO

Classical Humanism

CHAPTER FOUR

Classical Humanism in Outline

Is THERE or is there not a realm of law above the natural continuum discoverable to man? Does the law already exist, or does man make his own laws? The conflicting answers to these questions by the pragmatists and the classical humanists result in seemingly irreconcilable deadlocks involving basic cleavages concerning the nature of man's mind and the nature of the universe.

Outstanding in this controversial area is the question of ends. The Dewey philosophy strikes the classical humanist as comparable to a beautiful ship which sets out to sea piloted by an intelligent skipper who is unusually capable of steering the vessel into pleasurable waters and keeping it off reefs and shoals, but who is seemingly free from the obligation of docking at any specific port. He just sails hither and thither through the trackless seas without any goal. The main weakness of the pragmatist, says Jacques Maritain, is the exaltation of means over ends. Actually the pragmatic means are generally much better than those of the old pedagogues. The misfortune is that the pragmatist has lost sight of the end of education, and this is cause for great alarm.

These basic discords in education so intense today are really a continuation of a similar conflict which had already plagued the ancient Greeks. This sharp difference in thinking is highlighted by the debate between Socrates and the sophists. The main question: Is truth universal or relative? The sophists held that moral values are dependent largely upon the subjective reaction of the individual and that the utilitarian motive should be considered by the philosopher. These views the classic philosophers set themselves to refute, and so came into existence the matchless philosophical doctrines of Plato and Aristotle.

Classical humanism today considers its task analogous to that of Plato and Aristotle, responding to the contemporary call to rescue civilization from the same relativism which engulfed the ancients. Once again it is urgently necessary to discover those eternal principles which objectively substantiate the nature of the universe and of man, because as it is now, men "measuring themselves by themselves and comparing themselves among themselves are not wise."[1] Humanity cannot save itself without the rediscovery of the universal principles which undergird it. "As a fact," wrote Josiah Royce, "what you and I really most need and desire is not the new, not yet the old. It is the eternal."[2]

The times are critical, says Robert M. Hutchins, because men are no longer prepared to defend principles. Intellectual leaders, in fact, deny principles. Hardly anything remains but opinion, and everyone feels he is entitled to his own. There is no difference between good and bad, only between expediency and inexpediency. There are no morals, only folkways. Men are not different from animals, and it seems that the main aim of men today, as with animals, is subsistence and material comfort. "The only common principle is that there are no principles at all."[3]

The pragmatist in the twentieth century like the sophist in the fifth century B.C. (with a scientific evolutionary and biological support which the ancient sophist did not have) claims again that there is nothing settled in the universe and that uncertainty is the only certainty, that nature is constant flux and man himself is a natural product of this flux. The classical humanist today like the classical philosopher of antiquity flies directly into the teeth of such beliefs about the nature of the universe and the nature of man. The clas-

1 II Corinthians 10:12.
2 Gabriel, *The Course of American Democratic Thought*, 270.
3 Robert M. Hutchins, *Education for Freedom* (Baton Rouge, 1943), 90-93.

sicist argues that although nature is constantly changing on the surface, there is an inner immaterial reality which is eternal and unchanging, that above the world of sense there are eternal laws governing the universe. The order of the universe is discovered, not created, by man. Truth is therefore always the same, yesterday, today, and forever. It is within man's province to apprehend it, and this he does through the exercise of his reason.

Man's reasoning ability is not a product of biological evolution but the expression of the divine spark within man; it is the divine in him which exists above the natural flux, is "supernatural" even though immanent. By virtue of this immanent spiritual faculty a man may pursue intellectually the quest for the true, the good, the beautiful, the eternal and unchanging principles of the universe. It follows that education must primarily be concerned with the reasoning powers of man because these powers are what distinguish him from brutes. The mind of man is an immaterial reasoning faculty, and it is the major task of education to strengthen and to discipline this faculty.

For the classical humanist, the discoverable order in the universe gives man access to an authority which is clear-cut and unwavering. It is an authority which has developed through man's use of his reason, perennially searching for the principles of truth and dealing with the recurring problems of man throughout his history. This quest for truth has uncovered many principles which today as always are applicable and authoritative.

In the processes of education, therefore, it is not necessary to substitute the elusive element of pragmatic "interest" in place of traditional discipline and authority. The wisdom of the ages, in addition to its own intrinsic values, is an ever fresh form of discipline which sharpens the reasoning powers of the learner. In fact the pragmatic revolt against all manner of traditional authority is in essence the crisis in education today. The modern movement is the assertion that one attains the more abundant life by getting rid of the "don'ts." It is the peculiar responsibility of the classical humanist to reinsert into the educational realm a rational and proper authority which forestalls an otherwise inevitable chaos. Reason must counteract the present easy habit of adaptation to the influences of the changing environment by reassuring men that there are in the universe dependable and eternal laws by which they may govern and discipline themselves. The alternative is anarchy, which is the breeding ground of totalitarianisms.

That is why authority in the classical humanist view assumes such an important part of the educational program. Human nature insists upon some kind of authoritative ingredient in human society so that it may hold together. The classical concept of authority is the proper authority because it is truth in the form of principles rationally discovered. The subject matter is properly authoritative because it is the wisdom of the ages. The teacher is properly authoritative because he is disciplined in the wisdom of the ages. It is the aim of education, in this setting, "to see the vision of excellence . . . to get at least a glimpse of unchanging values of the eternal world."[4]

The classical humanist is gravely concerned with the pragmatic disregard for traditional authorities, especially in the light of the question to what authority do those in greatest power obligate themselves. (And today this question becomes more acute than ever, since men are endowed with greater power than heretofore known.) If men with power find themselves subject to no law higher than themselves, what is to happen? The parallel progression of an increasing power in the hands of men and an increasing relativistic concept about the control of such power leads to serious dangers, not the least of which is the eventual denial of the rights of minorities and individuals.

[4] Richard W. Livingstone, *Some Tasks for Education* (London, 1946), 50.

To speak of law and power easily involves the question of government. Both the pragmatist and the classical humanist are stanch advocates of the democratic form of government. But again their concepts of democracy separate along the same lines of disagreement about basic principles and ends. The concept of democracy which is supported by the pragmatist is of a Rousseauistic bent, equalitarian, wherein sovereignty resides clearly in the will of the people. It is this form of democracy which has become to some extent a pragmatic religion in support of some of the modern reconstructionist educational methods. Democracy in this sense is primarily a sharing principle involving all persons in all institutions, including the schools.

In contradistinction to this equalitarian concept of democracy the classical humanists subscribe to a form of democratic government, and an ordering of the whole of society, which specifically acknowledges the hierarchical element. Plato, Aristotle, and even Thomas Jefferson seem to share in the common conviction that a pure equalitarian radical form of democracy can only disintegrate into mediocrity, corruption, anarchy, tyranny. Society, according to the humanist conviction, even in its most democratic forms needs the guidance and direction of the elite. A progressive society needs a creative minority. Arnold J. Toynbee, the eminent British historian, refers continually to the creative element in growing societies which sets the pace for the masses which mimic. Jefferson, democratic though he was, insisted that leadership should be constituted of the natural *aristoi* who are best able to govern wisely and well. A democratically organized group does not by any means imply that just anybody governs, or that everybody equally shares in the process of governing. The intellectually elite should be assigned to the responsibilities of leadership, accountable, of course, to all of the people. In the final analysis the reason of the elite is judged more trustworthy than the general will of the people.

This same principle applies for the humanist in the educational scheme. Equalitarianism here too can only result in mediocrity. Therefore, the element of quality must be properly acknowledged in educational procedure. A proper understanding of the nature of man clearly shows him related hierarchically to the environment which surrounds him. Furthermore, his nature reveals within itself an ordered arrangement with the rational standing above the appetitive impulses. This description of the nature of man can hardly imply anything less than a hierarchical arrangement of his educational setup, in contrast with the equalitarian, radical form of democracy which seems logically to lead to a complete leveling of education. When this leveling trend becomes too widespread, it is the state which usurps the control and the power to make decisions as to what is good, politically and educationally, for the people. This kind of control by the state heralds the decline of any way of life dedicated to the principles of individual freedoms and rights.

Another area of sharp disagreement between the classical humanist and the pragmatist has to do with the emphasis on contemplation and activity. The pragmatist interprets activity as significant only as it involves the whole person, and the classical humanist interprets rational activity quite different. Since rational activity or contemplation is the highest activity of the educated man, the classical humanist considers the preservation of the cloister against the deluge of physical activity one of the most important tasks of education.[5]

One has only to look at the Middle Ages, says the humanist, to discover the tremendous spiritual power which was generated by persons who were interested in "being" even to the exclusion of "doing." Those groups cultivated monasticism and discovered hidden sources of spiritual power. Activity is obviously important, but activity can find its

[5] T. S. Eliot, *Essays Ancient and Modern* (London, 1947), 184.

proper aim and meaning much more effectively if it is correlated with times of withdrawal. The present danger is the trend toward unexamined activity, and it is the task of the classical humanist to reiterate the age-old knowledge that activity in the grosser sense must be balanced with the higher activity of the soul. Interaction with the environment and group activity are all worthy ingredients of the good life, but there is also the need for contemplation.

For the classical humanist it is important to outline a program of education which properly recognizes the need for "withdrawal" as well as "return."[6] An educational program should recognize the importance of activity in the pragmatic sense of the word, but it must lay even greater stress on the higher activity of reason lest action becomes shallow of meaning. Those who would be most effective in the world of action must first submit themselves to disciplines which develop the reasoning powers of the young.

The approach of the classical humanist to education is based on universal basic principles and ends, which supply the guidance necessary for the proper choices of means. Education must be concerned with activity, of course, but this activity requires knowledge of ends to be sought and means to be used. To discover the ends of education we must learn what constitutes the educated man. All education of immature persons must be subordinated to this end, because educational ends are concerned with the actualization of man's capacities. The primary factor involved in the educational fulfillment of man's end is the formation of good habits. Good habits lead to happiness, which is the final end of man. Good habits conform to the natural tendency of the human power they develop. Good habits are virtues. Virtues are the means to the ultimate—happiness.[7]

"Education is the process by which those powers (abili-

6 Phrase borrowed from Arnold J. Toynbee.
7 Greek point of view emphasized by Mortimer Adler.

ties, capacities) of men that are susceptible to habituation
are perfected by *good* habits through *means artistically con-
trived* and emphasized by any man to help another, or himself achieve the *end* in view."[8] There are certain truths,
either self-evident or capable of demonstration, about man.
One of these truths is that man is always everywhere the
same, and consequently the ultimate end of all men is always
everywhere the same. Therefore, good habits (the virtues)
are the same for all men, and education (the formation of
these good habits) is always the same everywhere for all men.

8 Mortimer Adler, "In Defence of the Philosophy of Education," in National
Society for the Study of Education, *Philosophies of Education* (Chicago, 1942),
209.

CHAPTER FIVE

A Greek Concept of the Nature of Man

How can we consider man's destiny unless we ask what he is? asks the classical humanist. For him more than for any other educator, perhaps, the nature of man is consistently a primary theme, because the purposes of education are fixed by the nature of man. Of course the classical humanist is by no means singular in his preoccupation with man's nature, for this problem is also central with men of sociological, psychological, and anthropological bent. For the classical humanist the safest way of escape from this contemporary whirl of intellectual and scientific crosscurrents is a return to the ancients, appropriating their wisdom as a foundation for understanding. To try to fathom man's nature is in any case a difficult task, and often philosophers have been lured into romantic or positivistic aberrations which lead to emphasizing some particular aspect of human nature. But again and again there is the return to the wisdom of the ancients with their time-tested approaches to this fundamental problem.

The pre-Socratic Greek philosophers, although they were primarily concerned with the discovery of general underlying principles in the physical world, provided important groundwork for an eventual Greek discovery of the significance of the individual. This new emphasis upon the importance of the individual appears remarkable against the backdrop of a widespread primitive viewpoint which understood the individual primarily in terms of the collective—the tribe or the community.

Following the pre-Socratic philosophers with their concern about cosmology, Greek philosophy moved toward a deeper concern about man himself. This concern was already being felt in many fields: in literature, in the new democratic political order, and surely in the influential teaching of a new group of philosophers called sophists. But the sophists made man "the measure of all things," and this relativistic outlook finally began to endanger the religious and social conventions of Greek society.

At this point Plato and Aristotle appeared to lead the attack upon the disruptive relativism of the sophists. Sophistic relativism assumed that all is flux and process, and that any God whatsoever to be found in that process is in it and not above it. The earlier myths in their naiveté were unable to withstand the deteriorating skepticisms of the sophists, and Plato set himself to the task of renewing the religious support of his society by refining its theological foundations through the discovery of the divine Universal.

Here is raised the question of whether the Greek humanistic concept of man was fundamentally anthropocentric or theocentric. It was Plato's purpose to rescue his civilization from the man-measure-minded sophists and to provide his culture with the highest end which was unchanging—God. But many men have held that in the end man himself—or rather man's reason—still remained the measure.

To make "God the measure" not only dignified man, since it gave a divine aspect to his nature, but also dignified education, because education (paideia) was cast for the role of developing man into the image of the divine. The true education was the path toward the fulfillment of the divine ideal—assimilation toward God. The Greek ideal founded education upon "God as the measurement."

This interpretation of the Greek concept of man relates closely, at first glance, to the Christian idea of man's creation in the image of God. Certainly it seems that both the Biblical and the Greek Logos stand opposed to sophistic relativism. Undoubtedly, however, there are radical differences in the Greek theology and Biblical theology. In the first place, with the Greeks man's reason is the basic means for the discovery of God, while in the Christian sense God discovers himself to man through revelation. In the second place, the God of the Greeks was a kind of "unpersonalized Logos" in comparison to the personal God of Christianity made manifest in the flesh through Jesus Christ. But in either case, man in the image of God, Greek or Christian, possesses a humanity which is not the essence of the natural world but of a supernatural order. Plato plainly states that the human race naturally partakes of immortality,[1] and Aristotle comments that "of all animals man alone stands erect, in accordance with his god-like nature and essence."[2] To this may be added the observation of Plato that men "imitating him [God] received from him the immortal principle of the soul."[3] Man is differentiated with rational "being" resembling the being of God the Infinite, and this is what makes man human. Man in his irrational state resembles the beasts; education cultivates his reason and brings him closer to the rational principle which is God. Though the Christian humanist is in one important sense at odds with the Greek emphasis upon Logos, it is quite evident that the emphasis on the transcendence of the spirit was a point of attraction between the humanists of both orders.

Returning again to the classical emphasis: Man is human because he is spiritual, and so he can be free, since the spirit, the immaterial, is not subject to the determinations of the natural world. Man's freedom inheres in his spiritual nature, and it is this freedom which dignifies him as a *person* who can think, choose, and will. Were this not so, he would not be different from the animals which inhabit the earth. To deny this spiritual quality of man's being is to reduce him to an enslavement by the world of things, by the collective body, by the changing whims of the times. This is not to say that man is not also animal. He is in fact a son of earth,

---

[1] *Laws,* Bk. IV, 721.   [2] *Parts of Animals,* 686a 29 (Oxford trans.).
[3] *Timaeus,* 69 (B. Jowett trans.).

but he is also a son of heaven because he is a *rational* animal. The body may be animal, but the soul is divine.

This belief that man is human because he is the bearer of divine reason leads to an exclusive emphasis in man's relationship to the rest of nature and to a hierarchical arrangement within his own nature. Because man belongs to two worlds, he has two distinct elements in his human nature: the body, which is identifiable with the senses, the passions, the less noble; and the mind, the reason, the divine, which is the more noble. And obviously for the Greeks the mind stands at the top in this ordering of man's nature. Reason in man must necessarily preside; reason sits in the driver's seat and directs the activities of the lesser faculties. If the hierarchy is deranged and the lower faculties gain control, man loses the truly human qualities of his nature. The animal part of man is considered accidental, temporal, particular, while the soul—the organ of reason—is the ground of his divinely constituted personality.

With Plato and Aristotle the hierarchical principle not only involved man's relationship to nature and man's qualities of mind, but also the relationship of man to man. Just as virtues were ordered into degrees of value, so society was ordered into classes. At the top were the philosophers, the elite, then the warrior class, then the tradesmen and the artisans, and at the bottom the slaves. Slaves had practically no political or social rights, and foreigners were thought of as barbarians. However, the Stoics later carried the ideas of Plato and Aristotle to more logical conclusions, teaching that all men possess the divine spark. This new concept of humanity leaped the boundaries of class and learning. Humanity became a truly universal idea. Once it was assumed that all men shared in a universal principle which made them human, the way was open for a spirit of cosmopolitanism and a trend toward humane ideals characteristic of classical humanism throughout the centuries.

The stoic concept of a universal principle which unites all mankind and supports ideal relationships between all men made possible a flowing together of Greek philosophy and early Christian theology, and these two streams later were joined in Thomas Aquinas, who synthesized the dominant features of Aristotelianism with the medieval Christian faith. Yet, according to Emil Brunner, the union of these two streams in Thomism was only apparent; there was throughout the Middle Ages a close association of Greek and Christian elements but never a truly inner fusion, mainly because at the source of each philosophical stream there existed a radically different concept of man's nature, as will be shown in a later section. With the Renaissance and the Reformation the two streams became again clearly distinguishable. The Renaissance was a renewal of the Greek ideal of the rational man, and on the other hand the Reformation, revolting against Scholasticism, reverted to the early church understanding of the personal nature of man in the light of his peculiar relationship to God the Creator.

The elaboration of the nature of man sooner or later involves the perennially difficult problem of evil and its relationship to man's nature. And any philosophy of education which pretends to be concerned with morality must also carefully consider this same perennial problem.

The Greek concept of the nature of evil is usually an emphasis upon the principle of privation or incompleteness of being. The source of evil is related to the idea of nonbeing. Evil becomes a possibility in relation to potential being which is not yet actual or complete. Evil, according to Aristotle, is not a necessary feature of the universe, but rather the result of the potential not becoming the actual.[4] And with Plato and his successors there is the implication that the physical body is evil as contrasted with the purity of the spirit. Man's evil is the result of the admixture of matter in

4 W. D. Ross, *Aristotle* (London, 1930), 178.

him.[5] Hence a soul and body dualism where the soul is good and the body, being matter, is evil, a tomb in which the spirit is imprisoned. A man overcomes his evil and his deprivation by partaking of the spirit. The divinity is of heavenly growth—whoever gets the divine element attains the perfect life. The confusion of the senses is finally overcome by rational control. The evil in man results from his deprivation of knowledge.

In the Thomistic synthesis of Greek philosophy, particularly Aristotelian, and the Christian faith, this idea of evil as privation or negation continued to be a basic tenet. The Christian philosophers, particularly Augustine, translated the principle of privation to mean a recession from a state of perfection as compared to the Aristotelian concept of evil as that which had not yet attained the ideal. Whereas the medieval Christian view conceived the privation of man's nature as a movement from the top down, the Greeks understood evil as an evidence of an incompleteness of the movement toward fulfillment from the bottom upward. In the Greek sense a man was the victim of his passions because his reason had not developed to the point where it could control the passions and rightly direct them. A man was evil in the medieval Christian sense fundamentally because he had fallen from grace, from his state of perfection in which he was created. In both cases, however, evil essentially was privation.

Today the classical humanists quite readily acquiesce to the basic interpretations of the Greeks, particularly Aristotle, in the assumption that evil is privation. Mortimer Adler states the matter simply when he says that the good is convertible with being, which in turn seems to imply that evil is somehow involved in nonbeing. This is one reason for the basic affinity between the Thomists and the classical humanists in contemporary education, though they may not

5 *Statesman,* 273.

agree on many points theologically. The rational activity of man reflects his divinity, and his irrationalities are evidences of his ignorance, of his incompleteness. The evil in man implies not necessarily *depravity* but rather *privation*.

The classical humanist today, although in some respects on common ground with the Thomists, seems in the final analysis to cast his lot in favor of a classical metaphysics as the rock-bottom foundation. Robert Hutchins in his book *The Higher Learning in America* observes that for the contemporary university, theology has been almost completely discarded. "To look to theology to unify the modern university is futile and vain."[6] This does not imply that theology should be degraded. The classical humanist should always respect theology. However, it is the Greek wisdom which offers the most consistent and surest support for the ordering of modern education.

For the contemporary classical humanist there is, then, in the final analysis that universal *within* a man which provides the measure of all things. The eternal divine spark within him, his reason, provides the basis for interpreting the ceaseless activities of life which continually engulf him. Man sharing the Reason of the divine Logos discovers the key to human existence. But the Greek discovery of God is a movement from within man to God, as compared to the Christian theology, for example, which holds that in the final analysis God discovers himself to man. In this respect there is involved a deep cleavage between classical and Christian epistemologies: the conflict between reason and faith, between believing because we know and knowing because we believe. Understood in this light the distinctiveness of classical humanism in the twentieth century is incisive in its relationship to orthodox Christianity, with which it otherwise shares a common conviction of the eternal and spiritual

[6] Robert M. Hutchins, *The Higher Learning in America* (New Haven, 1936), 97.

nature of man in opposition to the current naturalistic philosophies.

Classical humanism is dedicated to the idea that God is a spiritual principle and that this spiritual principle, active within human beings, distinguishes them from brutes. This divine principle in man provides the ends for man's education. Everything in nature aims at its own perfection, and so it is with the nature of man. Education is committed to the actualization of man the potential, man the ignorant individual, man the incomplete individual. The end of man is his highest humanity, his happiness, which depends basically upon the fullest development of the divine reason within to apprehend the ultimate good. Man's rationality insures his unchangeableness of nature and the consistent ordering of all his activities toward his ultimate and unchanging end. The means of educating him, therefore, determined in the light of the end of man (which is unchanging) may be quite graphically and clearly prescribed. Man is man by virtue of the divine reason immanent, and upon that norm educational procedures are built.

CHAPTER SIX

A Classical Solution to the Problem of Developing Responsibility

SURELY no phase of educational endeavor begins to compare in importance with the moral aspect of education: the ordering of a program in terms of what is right and what is wrong, of what ought to be and what ought not to be. Ironically, in the face of this ever profound problem, education currently seems hopelessly divided about the question of foundations for morals. At a time when education sorely needs a vigorous constructive approach to this problem, it finds its energies seriously dissipated because of its conflicting philosophies and ideals.

The present moment in history presents a unique hazard because it is a time when man possesses the technological means to destroy his civilization at the shortest notice, and all the while the basis of moral action becomes more and more beclouded, every man doing more and more what seems right in his own eyes. Educators must somehow rediscover and restate those universal principles by which men can lawfully compete with the tornadic impact of uncontrolled irrationality in the world. Already tragic is the insensitive disregard for those higher moral principles which through the long span of man's existence have been discovered as ultimates, unchanging, eternal. Unless there is a moral and spiritual revolution matching the scope of scientific and technological revolutions now taking place, civilization cannot be saved.[1]

1 The view of Robert M. Hutchins.

An extremely compelling evidence of the significance of the problem of responsibility in the contemporary world is the awful power now in human hands. Truly the scientists of the past two hundred years have demonstrated only too effectively that knowledge is power, but their works have also awakened within the hearts of men the growing conviction that power does not necessarily mean freedom, as was so hopefully supposed earlier, but more probably bondage in the end. The naturalist and the pragmatist have sponsored their progressive control over the powers of nature with supreme optimism, being motivated by their ideals of service to man (as superseding the earlier ideals of service to God), but unfortunately a mass of evidence lately accumulating shows that it is dangerous to confuse the will to power with the will to service.

The deeper ground of responsible human relationships was passed over too casually. It was not realized that power over nature also meant power over other men, that through the natural order of things some men always seemed to acquire more power than others, and that this implied not freedom but bondage for the masses.

When political power becomes ultimate, to whom does the person in greatest power answer? If there be no laws which stand above all men, why should any man in power consider himself answerable? These are but a few implications of the problems faced by a society which exposes itself to the dangers of moral skepticism; here lies a danger for an education founded upon revolt against traditional authorities. The philosophy of John Dewey, for example, radiates an assurance of progress: Knowledge is power, and power is freedom for all mankind. But his whole philosophy is energized with a faith in the natural continuum as the source of moral values. His views consistently exclude the reality, or even the possible validity, of laws which stand above men and nature. He has not presented an answer to the problem of obligation, and in the peculiar status in which mankind now finds himself, what could be more important? The pragmatic sanctions seem prone in actual life to succumb to the rule of expediency—an expediency often motivated by no higher objective than the accumulation of money and power. And why, realistically speaking, should this not naturally come to pass when men struggle for their existence in a world where expediency is the rule and spiritual realities are ignored? When men no longer consider themselves subject to higher moral or religious principles, there seems no longer an adequate defense against Machiavellianism. This is not to say that pragmatism lacks the will to do justice and to foster the spirit of brotherly love, but simply to point out that it does not possess the spiritual basis to fulfill its ideal. Pragmatism has grievously misunderstood the nature of man, and for this reason if no other, its position is insecure when confronted with the task of controlling men of power. And this problem of control and authority is, unfortunately, one of the most critical problems of the day. Pragmatism's peculiar weakness shows up at the point where only its greatest strength could suffice in the face of contemporary social and educational problems.

Educators must realize once again that the idea of what ought to be cannot be derived from the environment. The moral ideas of "must" and "must not" (responsibility) are unexplainable naturally. Whenever man is objectified, treated as not distinctive from the natural continuum, the principles of cause and effect destine him to act as does a machine, according to his construction, and then it is that the problem of responsibility is magnified a thousandfold. "Naturalistic determinism has not yet found a place for the concept of individual responsibility."[2]

In the light of the contemporary crisis, the educational calling of the classical humanist is clear. He, like Plato and

[2] Gabriel, *The Course of American Democratic Thought,* 381.

Aristotle, must restore the eternal and objective moral foundations which have been severely weakened by the sophistic spirit pervading modern life. Once again men must learn, and learn quickly, that truth is eternal and unchanging. Sensory experience which is the ultimate for the pragmatist is the starting point, not the end, of knowledge. Man because he is human does not remain within the sensory flux of life, but proceeds toward a knowledge of universals. Sensory knowledge is a means toward the discovery of the universal, the unchanging, the eternal. It is because man himself is the citizen of the eternal world, as well as the temporal world, that he can discover these eternal truths. He is the citizen of the supernatural world because he has within him the divine spark. Man alone can reason. Man alone can transcend the natural and contemplate in terms of ends, making choices. Man's very nature is a testimony to the truth that it exists above the flux.

And so man can know the true, the good, the beautiful, the universal; man does not need to order his society, his politics, his schools in the light of the changing climate of the various winds of opinion. By virtue of the fact that he is a man he has access to the truth, and he has but to discover the truth in order to learn that the truth will set him free.

Now it is obvious that all men do not address themselves to the arduous assignment of discovering the truth. Most men are generally occupied with the all encompassing task of making a living. Some persons have no higher purpose than to satisfy their animal appetites. For that reason, in a real-life society there is the establishment of law which governs man's individual and corporate activity. The laws which govern civilized societies are actually based upon man's rational discovery throughout the centuries of those eternal laws which govern the whole universe. Were men completely to discover the laws of the universe, they would be completely free. As it is, man is free to the extent that he is governed by laws founded upon the eternal. In any case the discovery and the appreciation of the proper meaning of law is the work of reason. Men as sons of nature are subject to passions and weaknesses of will; therefore they need the law, which becomes their schoolmaster. Eternal law becomes the rule for everyday responsible living, exercising men toward the greater use of their reason, protecting them from the irrational surges of their lower selves. Education becomes the discipline of children into the proper appreciation of eternal laws, and through this fundamental discipline they are given the spiritual framework for responsible relationships.

This concept of the law is an inescapable part of the well-ordered, well-proportioned society, and it is likewise an extremely important feature of the good school community. It is the realistic and reasonable means toward harmonious relationships between man and man. The young must learn the meaning of the law by habit. By rigorous, disciplined learning procedures which both shape and develop innate rational faculties, the young are refined to that rational level which frees them for responsible relationships with their fellow men. Through this discipline, by means of which the irrational and devitalizing passions which pervert the soul are subdued, the higher laws of reason are realized in the self, and men learn to be true to this higher self which they have discovered and likewise to be true to fellow sharers—all human beings, distinctive because they too possess the power of human reason.

Inasmuch as society always consists of its leaders and followers, the ideal education must serve them both, teaching both leaders and potential followers a knowledge and respect for the moral law through which society may be harmoniously ordered. The development of man's reason is the means by which he can be made to understand the law, to respect the law, to co-operate with the law. In the United States one of the amazing demonstrations of the inherent respect for law in a democratic people is the present attitude of Americans toward the Supreme Court. At a time when supposedly democracy is becoming radical, shifting the emphasis from permanent law to the changing will of the people, the Supreme Court of the United States is becoming almost a symbol of reverence. And yet it is of all tribunals the most remote from the people.[3] In spite of the view that pure democracy is only government by discussion, the Supreme Court continues to hold its prestige as a higher authority which proceeds in terms of comparatively fixed principles of law. Apparently Americans even in the twentieth century hold intuitively to the conviction that the higher law is more to be trusted than the changing will of the people.

The classical humanist firmly defends a twofold faith in man: that he can know rationally and that he can rationally support those laws which are necessary for the proper ordering of his society. The proper ends of man may be discovered by reason, and in the light of these discoveries men are capable of organizing themselves democratically through law. This kind of responsible relationship must be established educationally in the young. From infancy the child should be disciplined in the proper rational appreciation of the law—natural law, civil law, the eternal laws of human nature.

One of the consequences of pragmatism is the neglect of the necessary educational principles of discipline and limitation. The pragmatist, because he considers man a product of the natural world only, through necessity places a premium upon activity, because activity—interaction with the environment—constitutes his whole development; it is for the pragmatist the basis of the well-rounded person and the

[3] Gabriel, 406.

abundant life; it is therefore the essential basis of education. The broadened life is the enriched life; the life involving the greatest amount of constructive activity is the fullest life. The traditional concepts of discipline and limitation are set aside in favor of the more modern concept of "interest" in the widest possible range of activities.

This pragmatic interpretation of educational activity is misleading because it beguiles men to expend their energies trying to fulfill themselves within the natural continuum rather than trying to rise above it. According to the classical view the human spirit by its very nature cannot realize itself within the natural continuum. When activity in the naturalistic sense is made an end, the human spirit cannot but suffer the more intensely its incompleteness; this leads to even more intense activity in order to find a satisfaction which never materializes. Thus the round of activities becomes a circular process from which the soul cannot escape.

The claim of reason, on the contrary, is that the principle of limitation is the only saving principle in the world. "The more you limit yourself the more fertile you become in invention."[4] To paraphrase the Biblical quotation, narrow is the gate which leads to educational completeness, and wide is the gate which leads to educational shallowness and superficiality. The principle of "either-or" points the way to the high road; the "both-and" slogan is at best a circuitous route to mediocrity. "Restriction," says Dr. Whitehead, "is the price of value. . . . There cannot be value without antecedent standards of value."[5] Limitation, not excess, is the clue to the good life.

The application of the principle of limitation is a "must" at every level of educational procedure. This necessity of course involves the choice between goods. Even with the best-organized educational program the child cannot em-

---

[4] *A Kierkegaard Anthology*, ed. by Robert Bretall (Princeton, 1946), 25.
[5] Alfred North Whitehead, *Science and the Modern World* (New York, 1925), 178.

brace everything in its world. The educator must ever keep before his mind the proper end of man, and in terms of this end the educational program should be devised and limited. Since reason is the distinguishing faculty of man, reason must assume its foremost place in educational plans. Therefore the principle of limitation rightly applied points up the traditional rational disciplines of logic, rhetoric, literature, arts, languages, mathematics, history, philosophy, and religion.[6]

The schools of late seem to thrive upon the unselective accumulation of more and more materials of learning about more and more fields, which trend seems nothing less than an omen of a decadent and disintegrating civilization. Half education is a modern sign of the times—the result of a failure to realize the importance of the principle of limitation. This concept of limitation must be applied from infancy in order to develop virtuous habits, the right use of freedom. The person who limits his life finds his life. Limitation is the framework of freedom. "The free mind is first of all the disciplined mind."[7]

Through a proper program of intellectual discipline man attains human freedom, and human freedom is the basis of responsible activity. If man does not realize the fullness of the divine reason which resides within him, he becomes the victim of his lower nature. It is only by his reason which transcends these irrational forces that he truly becomes free, truly becomes human, truly becomes responsible; for responsibility is completely an alien concept to the natural world; it becomes reality only in the medium of a freedom which is the essence of the spirit. If man does not attain freedom, he is fixed by his lower nature as a machine is fixed by its construction, and with this turn of events one arrives at a virtual denial of human responsibility.

6 Livingstone, *Some Tasks for Education,* 17-24.
7 Hutchins, *Education for Freedom,* 91.

Victorious natural science with its observational and experimental methods has tended to obscure transcendent
values, for scientific research deals only with the sum of
things. But lately even the scientists themselves, along with
a multitude of serious-minded persons, are discovering that
scientific method does not by any means provide the whole
answer; that, in fact, the ancients were in some respects
more aware of the spiritual complexities of individual and
social life than modern man with all of his technology.
Modern Western culture has never really divorced itself
from the Hellenic roots which abundantly contributed to its
growth. Eternal Greece still remains, and the classical humanist argues that it is even now an intellectual arsenal from
which may be drawn powerful weapons to fight a winning
battle for the cause of democracy and freedom.[8] The prin-
cipal teachings of Plato and Aristotle can be used to infinite
advantage today in counteracting the same dangers of relativism which threatened Greek civilization. Virtue is vital
even for the modern scientific man. He who honors virtue
may have her, said Plato.

We must once again educate man rationally, so that when
he is asked a rational question he can give a rational answer.
"It is by this fundamental faculty . . . of giving a response
to himself and to others, that man becomes a 'responsible'
being, a moral subject."[9] The most important science of all
is the science of *choice*. This was the persuasion of the classic
philosophers. This was the scientific task of *paideia* (education). Education in the profoundest sense of the term, then,
was the development of responsible persons—persons who
make the right choices by virtue of the right kind of education which develops systematically their abilities to make

8 Richard W. Livingstone, *Greek Ideals and Modern Life* (London, 1935),
147-49.
9 Ernst Cassirer, *An Essay on Man* (New Haven, 1944), 6 (summarizing
the view of Socrates).

such choices in terms of the proper understanding of rightful ends.

The classical application of reason, law, and discipline result, socially, in a hierarchy. Any society, if it strives toward the true standards of justice, requires the ordering of law and justice in determining the rightful positions of the law discoverers, the law enforcers, and the law observers; there must be leaders as well as followers. When a well-balanced relationship exists between leaders and followers, justice prevails and the associations between the various parts of the society are responsibly harmonized. This is the ideal of proportion which applies not only to the society but to the individual person, for in him, also, reason must be dominant.

To speak of proportion is not to approve of the radical idea of equality. Distorted equalitarianism is a dangerous philosophy which in the long run destroys community. However pronounced this egalitarian trend is in the twentieth century, it is not by any means new. The Greek philosophers too were distressed with a strange warping of their cultural pattern wherein fathers behaved like children and became afraid of their sons; children acted like adults and stopped respecting their parents; teachers became afraid of their pupils, and pupils despised their teachers; the young tried to act old, and the old tried to act young; the egalitarian spirit seemed to pervade the atmosphere; even dogs, horses, and donkeys seemed to catch it.[10] These evidences are but the perennial symptoms of a society where man has lost sight of his true nature and his true end. The truly humanistic education needs to revive the meaning of proper hierarchy in society, supporting vigorously once again the standards of excellence and leadership, providing a way of escape from the numbing partiality to the "average," constructing once again the clear-cut standard by means of which a selection

10 Werner Jaeger, *Paideia* (3 vols., New York, 1945), II, 340-41.

is possible between that which is good and that which is not good. Man always has need of the unifying, proportioning power of Greek letters as well to know "the best that has been taught and said in the world."[11] Surely no one can deny the genius and the beauty of the Greek ideal of proportion: the proper relationships of reason and desire, of mind and body, of the well-ordered state with its rulers and defenders and artisans, all harmoniously related to fulfill the rational ideal of perfection. There seems always to be that creative, divinely inspired activity which strives toward the highest self-realization, spurred on by a passionate love for perfection.

Greek education is central to this classic ideal of proportion whether in the individual or in the society. When the individual soul is properly balanced and the state is properly co-ordinated, the society can best achieve its highest end. The young must be educated into this habit of personal proportion where reason rules and keeps the balance in order. The educational task is to defeat the blind powers of passion in favor of the wisdom of higher reason. When this purpose is accomplished, men in their various stations in society will display the proper respect for authority, law, and justice. In this manner all individuals in whatever station move satisfactorily toward the good life. The good ruler rules wisely and the good subject reacts responsibly to the laws which support justice in the society.

This principle of proportion—this justifiable hierarchy—applies with equal force in a social or communal unit. The leader committed to his special calling serves the welfare of all. The follower committed to his calling likewise contributes to the welfare of the whole. Reason provides for each the true understanding of the significance of his own position, whether it is that of leadership or followership.

11 Matthew Arnold, "Literature and Science," in *Essays and Poems,* ed. by Frederick W. Roe (New York, 1928), 57.

The proper ordering of communities, therefore, takes place within the framework of the law. Even on an international scale the only practical hope of responsible relationships between nations lies in the establishment of a league of nations by due process of law. Of course it is obvious that the law rationally formulated is not enough; it must be rationally respected. Reason, in one way or another, must take the place of irrationality. Men must arrive at the point where reason takes the place of war. Reason must conquer the passions. The problem of responsibility in personal relationships or in international relationships must be solved rationally, and there is no other way.

In the contemporary world, which is more and more yielding itself to emotion—a predictable outcome for a world which forsakes its faith in reason and law—the first and greatest assignment for the classical humanist educator is to establish dialectically those first principles which have been lost sight of. Once the true foundation has again been widely discovered, it may yet be possible to liberate this civilization from the hazards of its moral skepticism. This sure moral foundation must again be discovered by following the intellectual leadership of Plato and Aristotle, who competed so successfully with the moral relativists of their day. The philosopher today must again concern himself with the dialectical method. He must again become an explorer rediscovering basic rational principles and helping others to do likewise. The modern day is not tempered to theological dicta; the most effective approach to universals lies in the inductive approach which matches the philosophical bent of the times. The philosopher must begin with the sensory level of the skeptic and from there proceed to show that it is possible to distinguish between knowledge and opinion, that truth is objective.

Mortimer Adler in his articles entitled "A Dialectic of Morals" illustrates in some detail the actual framework of such a procedure by means of which universals are reached inductively in terms of sensory experience.[12]

Like Plato, Adler begins his argument on a ground common with that of the moral skeptic, assuming tentatively that there are no evidences of objective moral laws; everything is relative; there is no difference between knowledge and opinion. His first step is to show that no one denies the fact of preference and that the really essential problem is involved in the question, Is preference supported *rationally* or by the feelings? The skeptic of course will say that feelings are primary; pleasure and satisfaction are the basis for preferring one thing to another. The moral skeptic himself will agree readily that he is a hedonist. Pleasure is the greatest good.

Starting with this basic assumption the relativist will agree that the quantity of pleasure is involved in his preference. More pleasure is to be preferred to less pleasure. Now it appears that there are two criteria for preference involved— pleasure and quantity. Already the skeptic is forced to admit that a universal principle is involved for all men: A man *should* always prefer the greater good, in this case the greater pleasure. Now experience continually shows that men do not always choose the greater pleasure or the greater good. This universal assumption, therefore, is not merely descriptive; it is normative. It says what all men *should* do. To this extent the position of the skeptics is moral in a universal sense. If it be agreed that this moral judgment exists universally, it should tentatively be agreed that other such judgments could reasonably exist universally. But now to go a step further.

It appears that pleasure in itself cannot alone explain preferences. The object in itself seems to be related to preferences, supposedly because one object gives more pleas-

[12] The next paragraphs are a brief outline of Mortimer Adler's dialectic, which illustrates quite graphically Adler's proposed task of the classical humanist. The articles may be found in *The Review of Politics*, III (1941).

ure than another. Men desire a certain object, or good, because pleasure results from it. Men do not only desire pleasure for its own sake, but they desire objects which in a particular way supply pleasurable results. A careful consideration at this point will show that pleasure must often be distinguished from the object of desire. And furthermore, the "object" of desire obviously is to be distinguished from the desire for it. For example, a man desires wealth. The desire, and the wealth (the object of desire), and the pleasure derived from wealth are each to be distinguished from the other. Every object of desire should bring pleasure, but every object of desire *is not pleasure in itself*. Pleasure is simply one object of desire among many other objects of desire. Actually, men often desire unpleasurable objects in preference to pleasure. Hence, it becomes clear that the "object" of desire in itself has some bearing on preference. Pleasure as a simple criterion is most inadequate to explain preference. How then can it be reasonably explained that objects in themselves do indeed possess intrinsic value in relation to the preferences of human beings?

The answer to this question must be found in the nature of man. Various objects or goods (health, wealth, social goods, personal goods, and others) are only good and desirable because they relate to man's capacity to desire them. Because man desires them, they are good; man's desire is the force of his potential nature actualizing itself. Man is by nature everywhere the same, and thus man's universal nature objectifies the good of "goods." The problem then is rationally to discover the proper ordering of the process of attaining these goods. This proper ordering is to be discovered by rationally analyzing the end of man. The conclusion, to make Aristotle's long story short, is that the end of man is happiness.

Surely it is agreed that all men desire to live well, to be happy. All men *should* desire every sort of good which is an indispensable means to the end of living well. One could classify this statement as a universal in the moral realm. It is a normative law: Men *should*. . . . Actually they often do not. . . . The *moral* aspect is involved because men are qualitatively different from brutes. Men can *choose* objects in terms of ends. In other words, man can reason.

The end of man is always the same: happiness. Objects desired should be distinguished in terms of man's end: happiness. By means of reason man can understand his supreme end, and he can make his choices between the apparent and the real good. All men seek happiness; this is descriptive. Happiness actually comes through the *proper* seeking; this is normative. If man pursues his happiness on the basis of feeling—satisfaction of the senses—he fails; his failure stems from the fact that he desires as a brute. On the other hand, if man by reason understands his highest end and orders the means to that end accordingly, he fulfills himself as a human being. Only the proper understanding of the nature of man as a *rational* animal provides the means to the good life. The moral skeptic acknowledges happiness as the aim of all men, but immediately cancels out the means of attaining it by denying the objectivity of the end of man and the universal nature of man. It is man's nature to actualize himself, fulfill himself. Yet because man can choose, because he is free, he perverts his natural fulfillment by wrong thinking or weak willing. The objective norm for evaluating *human* desire (which is endowed with free choice) is natural desire, which is potency naturally becoming actual. The natural good is the objective basis for distinguishing between the good and the bad choices. The *natural end* of man is the criterion for directing his human choices. The natural end of man is happiness.

Moral training involves the formation of an "inchoate virtue"—moral habits formed by one person (who has rationally found himself) regulating the acts of another, this inchoate virtue providing the seed of genuine virtue. The legislator is the moral preceptor; just laws of the good society provide for virtue and happiness. The principles of law, dialectically developed and rationally supported, provide an important part of the solution to the problem of responsibility. The ability to choose between good and evil is a reasoned capacity, and therefore it seems quite evident that the highest contribution of the schools should be that of "concentrating on the reasoning essential to it."[13] This theme is neatly summarized by Everett D. Martin when he says that "there is only one sound method of moral education. It is in teaching people to think."[14]

The classical humanist, like the pragmatist, makes fellowship an important and significant part of his way of life. It is at this point, possibly, that the highest concept of responsibility, the idea of positive, unified, responsive relationships between persons, is most clearly circumscribed. Every person bears favor because he bears the name of man, according to Seneca. Man is man because he is the bearer of reason, and reason is a universal principle. The *humanitas* of the Stoics is the divine reason which unifies mankind as a whole. The sharing universally of the principle of divine reason binds together the whole human race. It is this principle which underlies Kant's dictum to treat all persons as ends and to act only in terms of the universal application of such an act. The ideal of *humanitas* implies a universal community of men and the cosmopolitan ideal of peace. Man's individuality is accidental and material; his spirit is universal. Hence there exists a cosmic sympathy which provides a noble foundation for world citizenship.

Irving Babbitt prefers the road of humanism even to the religious means of faith to create community among men. The secret to humanistic community is the common en-

13 Hutchins, *The Higher Learning in America,* 68.
14 Everett D. Martin, *The Meaning of a Liberal Education* (New York, 1926), 196.

gagement in the classical disciplines. Men in the common exercise and discipline of their reasoning powers develop a truly dependable ethical basis for social order and stability. In contrast to Christianity, which is not yet a world faith, the humanistic creed is not to be identified with any particular creed or religion and thus affords the most logical foundation for a world community. Robert Hutchins, too, shares enthusiastically in this conviction, assuming almost literally the role of a crusader as he travels up and down in the land recommending to all men the saving power of the classics, those permanent studies which offer the greatest hope of connecting man with man.

At this point the discussion could be turned easily to a practical educational problem which already has been posed for the pragmatist, namely, How, educationally, are the oppositions now existing between races in many American communities to be resolved? This current difficulty is as pertinent a question as could be posed in order to draw out the practical reactions of various philosophies of education in their solutions to a problem of developing responsibility which is now so painfully needed in American society. What then is the proposed solution of the classical humanist to this contemporary problem?

In the light of the discussion just concluded, the first phase of the humanist's answer is likely to be an emphasis upon the universalizing power of the rational disciplines. Sherlock Gass suggests that discipline, the exercising of all men in the same traditions of the great works of the past, giving the same elements, the same substance to minds, is the foundation of harmonious relationships between persons and groups regardless of how diverse their conventions and their outlooks. To forsake this discipline is to divorce men's minds one from the other.[15]

15 Sherlock Gass, "The Well of Discipline," in Norman Foerster (ed.), *Humanism and America* (New York, 1930), 284.

Now this is not simply a farfetched theory. One has but to observe the facility of adjustment on the college graduate level to the common participation in learning activities of different races even in universities located more or less in the center of racial tension in America. It appears that persons who have reached a comparatively high level of rationality, in university communities for example, adjust much more easily to interracial education than do those communities at large which have not yet reached this rational level. The eventual progressive rationalization of all segments of society will bear, the classical humanist argues, similar good results in the solution of this racial problem. And actually it appears that education is the key to the solution of this social problem.

This conviction is vigorously embodied in the missionary zeal of the contemporary classical humanists who literally go out into the highways and byways preaching the gospel of the great books program for all people. This program is actually an education designed for the common man. It is a movement seemingly vitalized by the burning conviction that the great ideas of the ages, if taken hold of by all peoples, will usher in that rational state of mind which shall literally save this world from destruction. Men thus shall be drawn together on the common ground of human reason, freely refuting thereby the irrational forces abroad in the land.

The simple logic of this position is that the proper relationships between one man and another man have an infinite number of times been established and assured simply through reason which effectively counteracts irresponsible relationships born of passion and appetite. It remains now for reason to prevail in group relationships, so that hate and war and passion are substituted on a grand scale by reason. Actually man has been struggling desperately in the past few centuries to make this substitution in the world at large.

From Grotius to Woodrow Wilson and the present United Nations program, the world has been trying to substitute reason for war in the ordering of man's society. Actually man has demonstrated the power of this theory. The union of the thirteen American colonies is a noted example of the victory of reason over irrationality in relationships between groups. At the present time the relationships between nations as well as the relationships between smaller groups have not been solved. Yet the road to solution is clearly demarcated. Reason must prevail.

The radical ideal of egalitarianism with its Rousseauistic irrational bases is utterly unworkable in real life. Higher and lower ranks, and authority and subordination necessarily exist in this life of reality. So the real problem is, What "quality of relationship" should exist between different classes and groups and positions in society?[16] The root of the unsatisfactory relationships between groups in society is not the result of hierarchy itself, but the lack of the infinitely valuable elements of self-respect and respect for others. Minority groups are not resentful primarily because of their position or their lot, but because they sense that they are used as means; they deeply realize that they are not respected as ends. This same significant psychological factor is often reflected in the reaction of soldiers facing the enemy. The one thing which most feeds the fires of resentment in their times of trial is not necessarily the agony of their lot, but the seeming callousness of their compatriots back home who live as if indifferent to their fate. This point touches at the heart of irresponsible group relationships and the disharmonies which result from them. It is simply lack of responsiveness to others as real persons, as ends rather than means.

To treat all men properly as ends is the burden of reason; it is the alpha and the omega of the rational mind, as sug-

[16] George H. Sabine, "Two Democratic Traditions," in *The Philosophical Review*, LXI (1952), 472.

gested by Kant. Once this rule prevails, it will be within the realm of possibility for all men to live in their station in life with a spirit of good will.

A society built upon the eternal principles of reason will flower into a well-ordered, well-proportioned hierarchy where men willingly coalesce and behave responsibly in the discharge of their activities. Men are equal to one another and treat each other as ends by virtue of the principle of a universal *humanitas;* on the other hand, men are communally bound together by the fact of their individual inequalities—which is substantially the true basis of community. Because all men are universally one in reason, they are drawn together; because men are different individually, they are united through mutual need of one another. This is the wisdom of reason; this is the positive, constructive contribution of reason. Reason in the negative sense facing the realities of life and of human nature recognizes the ever present irrational element in man: Man is rational, but he is also an animal. To the extent that the human community yields to the irrational impulse it must be governed by law. The law is the realistic authority which enforces order and right relationships between men when they have not yet found the autonomous power of reason freely to regulate themselves responsibly. Yet, even for the irrational man, reason is the only answer. Law is not enough. Until all men are disciplined into the insights of reason, there cannot truly be an ideal community. All men, whatever race or station, must be given the opportunity of discovering those eternal principles by which they become free individually and socially. For the classical humanist, *paideia,* universal education, is the high road to the good life rationally discerned—to the ideal fellowship between man and man responsibly ordered.

PART THREE

Educational Reconstructionism

CHAPTER SEVEN

Educational Reconstructionism in Outline

THE EDUCATIONAL reconstructionist is dissatisfied with the pragmatic progressive position which holds so insistently to its faith in a naive evolutionary progress as the means of overcoming the tragic abnormalities of the age. The ideal of a gentle and orderly progress educationally nurtured may suit eras of relative stability in society, but not the period of tortured transition which the world is presently undergoing. For different reasons the educational reconstructionist is also skeptical of the philosophy of the classical humanist with his cold reasoning in ivory towers, a procedure which can do little that is illustrious in the face of the rugged realities of a culture which must form a new world within the generally disintegrating framework of obsolescent institutions.

The reconstructionist makes no attempt to minimize the seriousness of the crisis which has gripped his culture. He is under no illusions about the critical bifurcations of a "schizophrenic society" in danger of actual dissolution as the result of its own deep-seated conflicts.[1] At moments of crisis, such as the world now faces, it is the extremes of the spectrum of theory and action which become accentuated. Issues become more clear-cut, requiring decisive response.

The reconstructionist is radical, not only in his estimate of the world's condition and in the means which must be used to get the world on the right course, but also in the goals which he contemplates in his vision of utopia. When the educational reconstructionist talks of utopia, however,

---

1 Brameld, *Patterns of Educational Philosophy*, 59.

he is well aware of the scores of utopian adventures in the past that have eventually proved illusory, fanciful dreams which did not take into account the realities of life and of man's nature. But this time, he argues, utopia is not another idealistic escape into the world of fancy, because science has revealed to the world enough knowledge to make the utopian dream an intelligent project, predictable, planable, controllable. The reconstructionist's utopia is based upon a vision of human intelligence socially directed toward the reorganization of man's life and world. In this contemplated transformation of society, education possesses the keys to the new kingdom.

The basic reason for the necessity of a new education is the inevitability of a contemporary trend called collectivism. "The modern development of man . . . shows one thing with indisputable clarity: the growing tendency toward collectivity and the invalidation of the individual. The trend toward collectivity is inevitable. We cannot evade it unless we set aside technical and rational progress—which is obviously impossible. Technics means collectivism."[2] What seems inescapably evident to the reconstructionist is the fact that the new world has become largely interdependent and that this new interdependency exists within the molds of outworn institutions constructed in the days when the world was not weighted with the current complexities resulting from dense populations, industrial revolutions, and the complicated problems stemming from the modern miracles of science and technology.

Most important of the traditional institutions which no longer coincide with the new way of life is the pattern of economics known as capitalism. Capitalism may have functioned tolerably in its heyday when world conditions were favorable to laissez faire and the world's untapped resources

2 Erich Kahler, *Man the Measure: A New Approach to History* (New York, 1943), 609.

gave free rein to individualistic ambitions, but the new world now largely exploited and inescapably bound by its industrialism and technics simply can no longer tolerate disrupting individualism in economics.

Collectivism is with us. No longer does the choice exist between individual freedom and collectivism, but rather between a collectivism dictatorially regulated and a collectivism democratically regulated. Education must realize this profound truth. Teachers should "recognize the corporate and interdependent character of the contemporary order, and transfer the democratic tradition from individualistic to collectivist economic foundations."[3] A new education is needed—a new curriculum, a new outlook for teachers. Failure to adapt society to the new technological world means death. It is a prime responsibility of the new education to face the implications of collectivism and to prepare for it. It must be recognized that the old capitalistic system is no longer adaptable to the designs of the new world and the new education. A first step in the recognition of this fact is the encouragement of a critical evaluation of existing economic systems; this is a necessary aspect of every person's education. This liberalization of the functions of education, namely the encouragement of critical examination of all existing institutions, seems the best hope for an eventual transformation of archaic economic systems into new patterns better adapted to the new world.

Now this introductory projection of economics as a phase of living significantly related to education seems immediately to call for a clarification of the educational reconstructionist position as related to other world views usually classified as radical or leftist in their basic assumptions. To attempt this clarification is difficult because educational reconstructionism is an emerging trend. One discovers an interesting

[3] Harold Rugg, *Foundations for American Education* (Yonkers-on-Hudson, N. Y., 1947), 577 (quoting Frederick L. Redefer).

but hard-to-define series of forward movements in the past twenty-five years, emanating mostly from the traditional pragmatic outlook. The earlier digressions from the progressive position did not usually extend too far afield, but some of the present radical reconstructionist ideas have moved quite far to the left and bear certain definite resemblances to Marxism.

In attempting to understand this leftist movement in education, possibly Sidney Hook's study of Hegel, Marx, and Dewey best outlines the basic reasons for certain underlying affinities between reconstructionism and extreme Marxism. On the other hand, a consideration of the educational reconstructionism of Theodore Brameld best outlines the fundamental differences between American reconstructionist radicalism and Marxist radicalism.

In the first place, it must be made perfectly clear that the Marxism of Marx is quite different from the communism of Stalin.[4] It is sometimes an extreme injustice to evaluate a man and his philosophy in terms of his successors, and this is especially true of Marx. Marx "stems from the liberal, humanitarian, democratic, radical traditions of Western thought. . . . He is a genuine, if errant, child of the enlightenment."[5] Once Marx has been legitimately distinguished from the corrupted Marxisms of the present, it becomes possible to understand some of the important likenesses of the philosophies of Marx and Dewey, an understanding fundamentally important to the reconstructionist whose American form of socialism is really dependent upon a synthesis of the strong points of Marx and Dewey. If the pragmatists would understand the original Marx and the Marxists would replace their outmoded dialectic with the scientific experimental method, their positions should converge, say the

4 Jim Cork, "John Dewey and Karl Marx," in Sidney Hook (ed.), *John Dewey: A Symposium* (New York, 1950), 338.
5 Cork, in Hook, 347.

reconstructionists, thus providing a strong foundation for the socialistic reconstructionist program.

The genetic likenesses of the two positions which make such a convergence possible are evident first of all in the common Hegelian heritage of both men. Both Marx and Dewey share a strong emphasis upon the organic nature of society and an insistence upon the elimination of a distracting dualistic interpretation of the nature of man and the nature of society. Both men retain the Hegelian idea of organic wholeness, but reject the spiritual nature of that "whole"; Hegel's Absolute Mind is replaced by Darwin's natural world of interaction and process. A natural monism takes the place of Hegel's spiritual monism. For Marx thesis-antithesis becomes primarily an economic problem; for Dewey it becomes the conflicting elements in a situation arising in the natural continuum.

This basic Hegelian idea of organism, applied to the natural realm as the only realm, leads to certain common conclusions about the importance of process. It leads to an agreement about the wholeness of man—that his mind as well as his body are the result of natural process and are actually inseparable. With transcendent realities eliminated from philosophy, it leads to a similar point of view about the practical nature of philosophy itself. Apriorisms are no longer meaningful; truth is relative; furthermore, faith and practice are not dual but a part of one process. On all of these basic ideas both Marx and Dewey reach similar conclusions.

Now in the second place it is important for the reconstructionist to distinguish the *differences* between the pragmatism of John Dewey and the communism of Marx. The crux of the disagreement is easily discovered in Dewey's devotion to experimentalism. Things could have turned out differently for the Marxists if they had not resorted to dogma and force as means of supporting their program. The

Marxists were brilliant in diagnosing the basic troubles of society, but they did not have the necessary democratic tradition to deal with those evils in an intelligent, experimental, and democratic manner. The tragic result is Russian communism.

It seems obvious that new forms of socialization and control are inevitable in contemporary society. Yet the socializing process is extremely dangerous, likely to end in fascistic or communistic totalitarianism. In the face of these hazards the best and most realistic plan is to apply the scientific method to the social problem and to do it democratically. The present socialistic answer is simply a practical extension of an earlier liberalism which freed the individual from feudalism and tyranny. Capitalism with its huge industrial empires has projected a new kind of tyranny inhibiting human freedom, and democratic collectivism provides the only emancipation from it. It seems in this changed world that the authority of capitalism is declining. The reconstructionist insists, however, that the authority of capitalism must be replaced by the authority of the scientific method, rather than autocratic dogmatic force of Russian communism.

So what really appears to be the foundation upon which the reconstructionists build is a theory of social democracy. While acknowledging their debt to Marx, social democrats believe the world requires the democratic support and the democratic methods outlined by John Dewey. Pragmatism is the guiding light which prevents the inevitable contemporary trend toward socialism from degenerating into communist totalitarianism. Dewey's whole democratic ideal is antithetical to Marxian force and violence. His faith is centered in an intelligent, democratic, experimental procedure which offers the best possibility of bypassing violence and forceful methods. Pragmatism consistently and diametrically opposes all kinds of absolutes, particularly the absolutisms of Marxism. Dewey himself wrote to an acquaintance, after publishing his book *Liberalism and Social Action,* 1935, saying that he thought he could be classified as a social democrat.[6] But consistently, in Dewey's views, the social aspects of life were always considered a means to free individual development.

The beginnings of educational reconstructionism in America are associated with the Great Depression. Its impact radically changed the point of view of some American leaders in education. The progressive educational philosophies supported by the teachings of John Dewey were in the twenties clearly individualistic, generally in harmony with the American capitalistic economic framework. Although Dewey had argued strongly for a greater acknowledgment of the social aspects of education, it seemed that the spirit of the times inclined educators to concentrate upon the elements in his philosophy which emphasized American individualism and traditional resistance to authority. The emphasis was still clearly upon competition and opportunity rather than co-operation and security. And educators shared the prevailing view that economic and social progress must be both inevitable and uninterrupted.

But depression and war shattered for many the worship of the free and independent spirit of individualism and the buoyant faith in progress. As always in times of stress and uncertainty, men began to re-examine their philosophies and institutions. George Counts was one of the outstanding progressives who raised serious doubts about the pragmatic opinions of his contemporary educators. In 1932, in a series of addresses entitled *Dare the School Build a New Social Order,* Counts challenged the progressives with these claims: (1) the progressives have no theory of social welfare; (2) they are not moved with strong convictions about the welfare of mankind; (3) putting their trust in a child-centered

6 Cork, in Hook, 349.

school does not take into account the new social crisis which faces society; (4) the pragmatic revolt against all imposed authority devitalizes the progressive movement; (5) imposition is inescapable in education. The author insisted that it was time for education to face the realities of life; it was time to reconsider more carefully the organic relationships of the school to community life and to face more squarely the practical problem of indoctrination in education.

Educational reverberations such as these in the thirties inaugurated the educational reconstructionist movement in America. The pragmatists at that time were becoming less optimistic about uncontrolled individualism and more intelligent about the social implications of education; they were also becoming more sensitive to the critical needs of their society for more clear-cut goals in order to offset growing uncertainties and confusions in society. Demiashkevich points out how William Kilpatrick in *Education and the Social Crisis* shifts from the position of "no goals in advance" to the concept of "cultural goals, socially established," toward which education must point.[7] Berkson insists that the reconstructionist development was already inherent but unemphasized in Dewey's recognition of the importance of the society. But Dewey's disciples were not as foresighted as the master; it required the humbling blows of bitter social realities to make them come to their senses and to make haste out of the far country of idealistic fantasies about uninhibited progress, and to readjust their views to the tragic social incompatibilities of their own world. According to Berkson, Kilpatrick's book, *Education for a Changing Civilization,* was an outstanding precursor of the reconstructionist movement. *The Educational Frontier,* a new periodical, shared substantially in launching the new movement. These earlier reconstructionists still held progressive and sometimes classical views which have since been sloughed

---

[7] Michael Demiashkevich, *An Introduction to the Philosophy of Education* (New York, 1935), 138.

off in the rapid advance to radical reconstructionism as outlined by such men as Theodore Brameld.

The main difference between the reconstructionist and
the progressive view is a matter of degree, according to Theodore Brameld. In both there is a common agreement that
the character of cultures is naturalistic, that cultural process
and change is the order of life, that there is no metaphysical
framework to the universe, that men create their own desti-
nies, and that there is no preordained purpose in history to
which life must conform. Indeed the universe is free, dynamic, expanding. But reconstructionism goes a few steps
further: The conflict between the "expansive" forces and
the "contractive" forces is universal, the expansive forces
being the struggle of the common man for freedom and the
contractive the efforts of the vested interests to hold their
advantage at the expense of the masses. This new social
concept is not only important but primary. Life must be
understood in terms of the social organism, and the diseases
which at present exist in this organism must be treated with
a radical kind of medicine. The pragmatic concept of the
world and of man is dynamic and promising, but the pragmatic weakness lies in its stubborn denial of preordained
goals, in its continued rebellion against authority, and in
its blind faith in progress. So long as pragmatism rejects
the ideas of goals and authority, its vitalities are neutralized.
Pragmatism has force and method, but nothing to lead it to
act boldly and vigorously. The kind of world men live in
today requires this boldness of action, and reconstructionism
provides the necessary blueprint for a brave new world.[8]
There are sharp differences between the democratic individualists (the earlier pragmatists) and the democratic col-
lectivists (the later pragmatists). The reconstructionists
have moved quite close to the Marxists in their radical social
interpretations of society, their strong condemnation of the

[8] Brameld, 720-24.

evils of capitalism, their inclination to name economics as the cause of social evils, and their conviction that clearly outlined goals are necessary. Yet the modern reconstructionists do not subscribe to dictatorial power in the hands of the few but to power established democratically through the co-operation of the masses—to democratic social power as opposed to autocratic power. To these ideas, however, the earlier pragmatic individualists are still hostile.

The reconstructionist tends to lose patience with his compatriots, the earlier pragmatists. Theodore Brameld, deeply moved by a world "blotted with the grim realities of fear, deprivation and blood," accuses the progressives of limiting education to an innocent form of feeble individualism. The progressivist seems to avoid commitment and conviction; he avoids the problem of the future; he does not possess enough of the crusading spirit; he is still entangled with the traditional concept of individual evolution rather than social revolution; his outlook lacks cohesiveness and purposiveness; he has no clear authority upon which to build; he is still "caught in the false individualism of disintegrating Protestantism."[9] The pragmatist makes a fetish of method so that it becomes an end in itself which leads only to confusion and uncertainty. He confuses "planning" with the "planned." Of course, planning is basic to the educational program, but it is ineffective if there is no definite goal. Reconstructionism completes the pragmatic ideal by recognizing not only the process but the goal.

The educational reconstructionists are thoroughly in accord with the claim of Ross Finney, who said that educators are not only running the schools, but they are running the world. The school, he said, should supply the pattern for the whole of society. Later sociological and psychological discoveries have borne out clearly the significance of Finney's remarkable sociological insights. Today the school has in-

9 The observation of Alexander Meiklejohn.

deed been discovered at the center of the social vortex, in a position to give reconstructive direction to the whole of society in its throes of transition.

It seems that sociologically and psychologically the twentieth century provides the perfect stage for the anticipated drama of the emancipation of the common man. All over the world there are the vibrant expressions of the reconstructionist spirit as exemplified politically in the socialist movement in England, the Scandinavian co-operative experiment, the upsurge of the colored races in America and elsewhere, the significant expansion of Russian communism, the rapid growth of labor movements, and the resurgence of youth, especially in Oriental countries.[10] The reconstructionist must harness these expanding forces, join them, use them, direct them. Education must provide the framework. Education must take the lead.

Educational reconstructionism is not at all hesitant in admitting the necessity of a religion to motivate and empower its program. The unrational element in man's nature is powerful and useful and necessary. An educational program which does not take into account the power of faith and religion is virtually defeated before it gets under way. For this reason there must be certain religious features in the reconstructionist pattern, motivations which support a dynamic faith. The traditional American faith underlying education was the Christian faith in God. But the eighteenth, nineteenth, and twentieth century intellectual and scientific impacts have all but obliterated this Christian faith, and a radical democratic faith is taking its place. In the past three hundred years there has been a definite transition from the control by the church to the control by the government in many fields, and particularly in education. As the state takes the place of the church in education, it must develop its own new religion. Obviously that religion

10 Brameld, 391.

is democracy, the religion well adapted to provide a dynamic faith for a reconstructionist program. It was the religion of Rousseau with his vehement crusade for equality. Such a religion gives men the will to expend their lives if necessary for the cause. For Rousseau the general will of the people takes the place of the will of God. Man no longer has a divine protector. His rights are established by the state, and the state replaces the church as the primary institution of human brotherhood. The Rousseauistic state is the non-theological substitute for medieval theocracy. This is the reconstructionist radical democratic alternative to Russian communism bogged down with its cult of autocracy. The majority is completely sovereign and determines what it is that men want, what their commonly agreed goals are. With the democratic power of majority will, those goals are irresistibly achieved.

Brameld has daringly planned the transformation of society through education. The framework for the reconstructionist education in all levels of learning, he says, shall be group discussion, testimony, consensus, and commitment.[11] Education must join itself to the expansive forces in the world which are struggling for the freedom of the common man. The first practical step of education, in this respect, is its affiliation with trade unions. These unions offer an excellent opportunity for a central channel through which the schools can fulfill social goals for the community. A general outline of the reconstructionist blueprint suggests an economy of abundance, a service state, a cultural design for the emphasis on the artistic in all phases of life, an educational system which is centralized and free to all, universal education from the nursery to adulthood, an education using all media of propaganda, a humane order which responds particularly to family life and to the needs of old people, minority protection, and world democracy.

11 Summary of Brameld's views in *Patterns of Educational Philosophy.*

Since education becomes a "single great cultural design" of economics, politics, art, science, and human relations, there would ultimately come the necessary discouragement of private and parochial schools which promulgate divisive doctrines of vested interests and weaken the will of the majority.

This, briefly, is the story of the inevitable advance of ideas and practices in a dynamic society. History is replete with the illustrations of the conservative-liberal-radical movement. It is the story of the theists, followed by the deists, followed by the atheists. It is the story of Comenius, who conceived of both man and the state created by God; followed by Locke, who compromised and said the state belonged to man and the individual belonged to God; followed by Rousseau, who said both the state and man belonged to men. It is the story of William James, who said God was allowable for men who empirically benefited from a faith in Him; followed by John Dewey, who said the concept of God was generally impracticable and should be ignored; followed by the reconstructionists, who say definitely that the traditional concept of God is itself a kind of vested interest and should be eliminated as expeditiously as possible in order to unblock the channels of progress. This is the pattern in history which provides the utopian reconstructionist with great hopes for the future of his movement as he presents his blueprints for a new society and a new world.

CHAPTER EIGHT

A Social Concept of the Nature of Man

THE RECONSTRUCTIONIST is convinced that one of the critical weaknesses of contemporary Western civilization is the cult of individualism. Both ancient Greek humanism and modern Christianity have helped develop an individualistic trend in almost every sphere of human activity—in philosophy, religion, science, economics, politics, education. The result has been an unnatural isolation of the individual from his neighbor, accented more than ever by the machine age. Now finally there is evidence of a strong counter movement toward a new understanding of the social nature of the individual, a new appreciation of the necessity to interpret the individual in the light of his society and his total surroundings.

In America, at least, the eighteenth and nineteenth century educational perspective was strongly colored by the atomistic concept of man, largely an English influence, which appropriated nineteenth century biological and psychological discoveries to support it. Spencer, for example, utilized the Darwinian evolutionary principle to support an individualistic philosophy in education. Likewise, the new science of psychology was at first mainly involved in the error of trying to understand the nature of man in isolation. It is understandable, therefore, that the earlier progressives, John Dewey for one, emphasized the individualistic spirit in their child-centered education.

The modern social concept of man's nature has much in common with pragmatism, just as does educational reconstructionism with progressivism in education. In the first place they are joined in their mutual insistence that man is completely a product of the natural continuum. According to Sidney Hook, the concept of the soul as supernatural is a Christian idea, and the classical humanists have borrowed this concept from Christianity. But whether this supernatural concept is purely philosophical, based on reason, or theological, in the sense that it is based on revelation, it cannot in either case stand against the critical scrutiny of modern science and associated contemporary philosophies.

The modern philosophical principle that "process" rather than "being" is the ultimate principle of the universe has the most profound implications when it is applied to human nature. Man is not an absolute being whose nature is always the same, as the classical humanists believe, but is rather an evolving entity, developing into what he is through interaction with his environment. Man increases in value to the extent that he interacts successfully with a good environment. This is one of the basic presuppositions of Kurt Lewin. Man is no longer understood in isolation but in terms of "individual and the environment." The emphasis shifts from the organism to the process. The question of relationships becomes the dominating consideration. In this principle both the pragmatists and the educational reconstructionists concur.

Once human nature is relieved of its theological and metaphysical a priori straitjackets, it is possible to appreciate man's remarkable plasticity and potentialities for development. What really fires the imagination of the reconstructionist is the understanding of man as unlimited in his possibilities, especially since modern science has made great progress in setting up techniques to control the interaction of the organism with the environment. What science has done in the control and direction of inanimate nature has been an excellent preparation for a new challenge as it now turns its attention to the greatest problems of all, those concerned with man and his society in these troubled times.

A further important liberation of the nature of man, as

he is understood in the light of biological, psychological, and sociological empirical investigations, is the final removal of the theological doctrine of sin, especially original sin. Since the Reformation there has been an interesting advance philosophically in reference to man's nature and sin. John Calvin was the leading exponent of the doctrine that the evil in man's nature overcomes the good. Jean Jacques Rousseau reacted sharply to this harsh doctrine and argued that essentially man by nature is good. Rousseau concluded that vice and error are strangers to man's constitution; they are due, in short, to his institutions. Were it not for vested interests unresponsive to man's highest good, his beneficent inclinations would "gush forth torrentially." These views are basically the position of the present educational reconstructionist, except that he would be inclined to carry the advance one step further by saying that scientifically one must describe human nature as fundamentally neither bad (Calvin) nor good (Rousseau) but neutral, which also is the carefully considered opinion of John Dewey.

The reconstructionist is more realistic than the progressive in his recognition of the evils of society, but he is consistent with pragmatic interpretation in holding that the evil does not lie within man himself. Indeed, man has undergone a kind of "fall," according to the reconstructionist, not in the Christian sense of original sin but in a social sense (if one takes Karl Marx or Rousseau seriously), when he became civilized and embarked upon the capitalistic way of life. Society is in a state of revolt, and therefore man, because he is the product of society, is against himself. Sin is not the defective "being" of the humanist, or the incomplete "intelligence" of the pragmatist, primarily, or the Christian concept of a perversion of relationship of man to God, but simply a badly adjusted environment distorting the plastic, responsive, sensitive human organism. Social institutions, not men, are bad. John Dewey in this respect justifies the special place which the reconstructionists allow for him in their program when he observes that the defects of society "do not lie in an aversion of human nature to serviceable action, but in the historic conditions which have differentiated the work of the laborer for wages from that of the artist, adventurer, soldier, administrator and speculator."[1] At another time Dewey observed that social conditions rather than an "old and unchangeable Adam" are primarily responsible for wars. George Counts states simply the conclusion of the matter in a positive sense: The good person must be formed in terms of a good society, and a good society is not natural; "it must be formed by the hand and brain of man."[2]

The reconstructionist shares with the pragmatist a fierce kind of loyalty to the Rousseauistic ideal of equality for all men in reaction to the classical and frequently Christian patronage of the hierarchical orders. The doctrine of equality supplies a driving, almost evangelical motif for the reconstructionist because it is at this point that he can most effectively appeal to the masses in bringing about a reconstructed world. There is no argument which can more completely activate the expansive forces of the common people than to emphasize the inequalities they unjustly endure. There is no longer any doubt that men are essentially born equal; reason supports this thesis; science continually demonstrates it; nature decrees it. If men are in truth equal, they all deserve the enjoyments of the good things this life offers, which until now have been denied the masses by vested interests.

To subscribe to the tenet that all men are equal does not by any means imply that there should be a leveling down of society; rather, there must be a "leveling up" of the population. The fact that all men are born equal implies

---

1 Dewey, *Human Nature and Conduct,* 124.

2 George S. Counts, *Dare the School Build a New Social Order* (New York, 1932), 15.

that persons with outstanding abilities and opportunities should not use these personal prerogatives for themselves, but dedicate them to the welfare of the group.

Once it is agreed that the nature of man can only be properly understood in terms of his total "gestalt" or "life-space,"[3] the entire field of time and space is understood as contributory to the significance of the individual. Now the social scientist must try to understand the basic principles of this total field which bear most directly upon the formation of human nature, or more particularly, human personality. The educational reconstructionist is inclined on this point to agree with Karl Marx that the area of economics is the starting point for reconstruction because it bears vitally upon the whole structure of society. To make economics the starting point by no means implies a crass materialistic interpretation of life, but simply that the ideals of human freedom and human equality can only be fulfilled when material needs are met, and this can only happen when the aberrations of a capitalistic society are readjusted so that the individual is free to fulfill himself intellectually in an atmosphere of social harmony. The end of this program is not the accumulation of material goods but the emancipation of the human intellect. This too was the goal of Marx. The main reconstructionist disagreement with Marx is his method of reaching the goal. Violence and autocratic dictatorship have backfired. This method must be replaced with a saner democratic process of majority group action.

The educational reconstructionist also distinguishes himself quite definitely from the traditional pragmatist in his serious concern with the irrational nature of man. The pragmatists are inclined to put the supreme emphasis upon the power of intelligence to eclipse these irrational features of man's nature. Some of the newer thinkers point to "instinctual and emotional forces" which eclipse the forces of

3 Kurt Lewin's terminology.

intelligence. Again, dependence upon one's intelligence suggests individualization. For the reconstructionist, education must become more social and less intellectual in the individual sense of the word. A fuller understanding of man's nature cannot help taking into account the dominant role of the irrational, or the "unrational" as Brameld prefers to call it. Man is basically a goal-seeking animal, and much of his goal seeking is "unrational." In addition to acquiring knowledge by "apprehension" (intelligent learning), man also possesses a "prehensive ability," profoundly enhanced in group interaction. The group mind tends to be "prehensive," possessing a kind of intuitive, emotional, instinctive faculty by which it discerns the really deep things of life. This emotional side of man's nature the pragmatist has overlooked. In order to challenge men to reconstruct their society, the emphasis upon intelligence is not enough. The whole man must be appealed to, and this includes in no small degree his emotions. The irresistible force upon which the reconstructionist depends to reach his goals is the emotional, unrational prehensive flow of the group mind, guided in the proper direction by the social techniques which insure democratic procedure in the reconstruction of society.

Some of the educational reconstructionists, notably Theodore Brameld, are inclined to follow the Marxian pattern, centering their educational efforts upon a transformation of the economic framework as the primary means of fulfilling the new order of society. There are, however, other vanguard sociologists and social psychologists, for example, Mannheim and Lewin, of reconstructionist temper who do not wish to stop with economic considerations only. They point out that in so doing there is danger of an overemphasis upon one aspect of man's nature and man's world to the exclusion of many other factors which also must be dealt with in order to carry out a successful program. In other words, the sociological emphasis of reconstruction is total. And this is to say that the economic sphere does not account for the whole nature of man; we must consider all of the cultural factors which contribute to his nature. Since the person is the product of his society, and since sociological advances have pointed out the infinite possibilities of social control, the time is at hand when the ideal for man can be selected, and he can be sociologically developed into it. Behaviorism, one of the older psychological naturalistic interpretations of man's nature, suggested surface planning— really an external approach—whereas the newer reconstructionist ideal for planning envelops not only externals, but the whole man. Kurt Lewin in his field theories gives eloquent support to this new ideal. Psychology attempts to understand all of the underlying realities of man's nature scientifically, just as science deals with the problems of chemistry and physics. The whole field affecting human behavior becomes the ground for study, including not only the physical world, but the psychological and social world as well. The scientific outcomes of such investigations point to a whole new control of man's future, of his society, even of man himself.

These new perspectives in psychology and sociology provide an educational framework (psychology and sociology are becoming more and more the foundations of educational theory) for the reconstructionist platform. New cultural factors must be built into personalities. A new kind of world requires a new kind of person. This assumption presupposes a new kind of education which is predominantly social. The educational program must be extended into the community in order to create social patterns which in turn sustain the new social personality. Reconstruction must take place in mass, group, form. The traditional concept of "individual conversion" is outdated. The "transformation of the individual in order to transform society" idea should be reversed, and the new procedure should follow the plan of converting the society in order to convert the individual. Man's repressions and individual perversions must be understood socially. Once this is accomplished, the planners can decide what is ideal for man's new nature and reorganize his environment accordingly. Public education in the twentieth century provides the ideal means for the execution of this program. Of course a consideration of this kind of mass regulation of the mind of man is frightening, but from a realistic point of view it is inevitable. Therefore the educator must take these sociological tools with all their potencies and see to it that they are used rightly.[4]

In the final analysis, man is but one segment of nature's infinite expanse, and what science has already done in its conquest of plants, animals, soil, and water, it can do to improve the nature and destiny of man. When Finney said that educators not only administer schools but the world, his observations were couched in an idealistic, traditional perspective. Now the educational reconstructionist speaks the same language with the realistic backing of scientific knowledge adding tremendous conviction to his assertions that the transformation and direction of youth are the keys to the world's major problems.

4 See Karl Mannheim, *Man and Society in an Age of Reconstruction* (New York, 1941).

CHAPTER NINE

A Radical Solution to the Problem
of Developing Responsibility

Surely no one can be more serious about the problem of responsibility than the educational reconstructionist, although with his dynamic concept of the role of education in society he shifts the weight of responsibility from individual to group. He recognizes the gravity of the present trend toward the magnification of power in the modern world and what this trend implies in reference to the responsible application of this power. In a simple society, man cast himself upon the mercy of some inscrutable higher power. But now man realizes he must take the place of the gods because he himself possesses the knowledge and the control formerly attributed to them. He, not some higher mystical power, must act, plan, control. To avoid this new responsibility is nothing less than criminal, for if man does not actively direct and control these new forces, they will crush him. History is rushing toward a decision between the forces of expansion and the forces of contraction, between the forces of freedom and tyranny. Men must choose between them. How they choose decides the fate of civilization; it is a choice, possibly, between life and death. The forces of expansion are evident in the awakening of common peoples the world over, "mingled together in a vast rumbling, clumsy, infinitely powerful mass of hundreds of millions of men, women, and children; blacks, whites, yellows, Jews, Christians, Mohammedans, peasants, professionals, laborers, artists, doctors, teachers."[1] These forces may liberate the

1 Brameld, *Patterns of Educational Philosophy,* 669-70.

world forever from the tyrannies of special interests and traditional monopolies. There can be no doubt that it is the school's task to harness and to direct these potentialities for liberation. This is one of the grave and overwhelming responsibilities of education.

The current problems of society are so serious that the older concepts of individual responsibility are no longer adequate for the immense tasks of social reconstruction. The new emphasis upon responsibility must be social. The deep-seated ills of society require the concerted power of the group to remove them. The progressives with their program centered on the individual pupil had not taken into account the possibility of radical and total social disintegration. For that reason, among others, the progressive schools with their enthusiastic experiments now show serious signs of disintegrating morale and poor discipline. Undoubtedly the home is also shirking its responsibilities in training American youth, and probably there are many other reasons for the plight of our young people, but their condition today points up acutely the need for the new education. The teacher as an individual no longer can cope with many of these problems, because they stem from a total social disintegration. The logical answer is a social approach. The restoration of order and stability in the schools can only be accomplished by a social program strong enough to direct and to regulate this shattering individualism which is sabotaging the social good. Actually, the teacher should not be the center of an educational program; his learning, personality, and authority are not the basis for good educational procedures, as the humanists believe, but rather his ability to manipulate the social environment in such a way that *social* pressure is brought to bear upon the individuals of the group in order to develop responsible action. Thus the educator creates a social and cultural field which properly supports and influences the individual in his choices between responsible and irresponsible actions.

This implication of the "social" concept of responsibility suggests the need for a revised set of values for mankind. The rules by which men lived for the last two or three centuries are now outdated. A new interdependent society requires a new, socially oriented set of values. The admonition "love your neighbor" now connotes a much greater social significance. Men now need "a set of attitudes and ideas by which to tell what is right and wrong, desirable and undesirable, with respect to the policies and actions of large social groups that have supplanted the old-fashioned community."[2] Ethical standards should be discovered to a greater extent in social relationships. Moral choices are more to be determined within the social setting. The question of moral man is less significant than the problem of immoral society. Twentieth century problems are centered in mass movements and mass relationships.

The path to new concepts of social morality, according to the educational reconstructionist, lies in the techniques of social consensus, a discovering of the group mind. This involves an inductive procedure wherein consensus, agreement through public discussion, extends outward through larger and larger groups until there is a majority agreement on basic issues in the whole country, or even in the whole world. The establishment of a proper set of values starts with an examination of individual wants and proceeds by intensive investigation of the larger needs of the community. The majority agreement on basic issues is not just a quantitative result—a counting of noses—but a qualitative result as well, for the sources of consensus are the prehensive, unrational, deep desires of all mankind, and consensus so supported becomes the standard of value by which the society regulates itself and makes its social decisions. The idea of power "becomes itself a moral concept of mass action through

2 B. Othanel Smith, William O. Stanley, and J. Harlan Shores, *Fundamentals of Curriculum Development* (Yonkers-on-Hudson, N. Y., 1950), 57.

democratic channels for Utopian goals."[3] Power, the greatest of which is the over-all group mind centered on its goals, becomes responsibly directed because it is applied in accord with the wants of the majority discovered democratically.

The starting point for the discovery of values is the "wants" of individuals. A human being is a goal-seeking animal. Learning what his goals are involves a "consensus" process, and this process needs no superexperiential dictates. The process is social; the individual no longer possesses the means to cope with the immensity of social problems, and he also lacks the breadth of understanding as an individual to determine values. Power and values alike belong to the collective will which democratically discovers its values and applies its powers. The highest value which man can know, the final all-embracing value, is the supreme ideal of "social-self-realization." The individual in a prehensive and unrational kind of way identifies himself with the group mind in the processes of social consensus and thereby realizes his deepest wants. A person by denying himself individually finds himself collectively; this is "social-self-realization." This is actually not a novel concept, because it was long ago anticipated by the Christian emphasis upon the dignity of personality and the brotherhood of man. In fact this whole group process with its emphasis upon the unrational and the prehensive readily submits to a religious impulse which is admittedly essential to the human being. A new "cultural myth" becomes the basis for religious faith, although it is a faith grounded in modern scientific knowledge.[4]

The educational reconstructionists, like the classical humanists, are vitally concerned with the problem of freedom, for therein is also fundamentally involved the problem of responsibility. No one seems to disagree with the assumption that responsibility implies freedom and freedom implies responsibility. The reconstructionist, however, in contrast to

3 Brameld, 506.   4 Summary of Brameld's outlook.

the classical humanist, places a quite different interpretation on freedom and responsibility.

A realistic survey of the current social problems will easily show why new concepts are necessary. The complexity of modern society's problems cancels out any hope of individual mastery and with it the high place of individual responsibility in the face of such problems. Social forces are thus inevitable. The individual must limit his own freedom to enhance the freedom of the group. The social force established in free groups makes possible the more satisfactory control of invidious forces in the world with which the individual cannot cope. In the modern collective trend the individual is becoming less and less free; as an individual he is in the grip of circumstances about which he can do little. Man's best hope, therefore, is a collective effort to re-establish freedom for the group. It is the group, really, which is free and which discovers itself increasingly accountable. Social responsibility is gradually replacing individual responsibility. The classical humanist's emphasis upon individual responsibility, noble though it has been, is now outmoded by new needs for collective responsibility.

For the reconstructionist the modern complex culture necessitates the subjugation of the individual to the group. Submission to the group makes responsible action possible. The group is responsible because it is free and capable of responding to the whole situation. The complexities of modern life make it difficult for the individual to respond to the total situation or to act effectively in the face of it. The freedom and the responsibility of individuals must be realized in the obedient act of conforming to the group mind—a democratically determined group mind—and in the group, men realize their true freedom; they fulfill their deepest responsibilities. Intelligence can emancipate education, and for that matter the whole society, not by acting individually but by discovering socially the necessary road which must be followed. This road can be discovered democratically, through public consensus educationally directed, in order to fulfill the new ideals of social freedom and social responsibility. And finally, where the individual is faced with crucial decisions, the group interpretation of what is necessary is the safest and most satisfactory.

The reconstructionist, in contrast to the progressive, deals realistically with the problem of authority. He does not, like the pragmatist, undercut all foundations for authoritative action in the face of radical difficulties. The reconstructionist feels with the pragmatist that he can no longer appeal to the will of God to help him with practical decisions. Neither does he wish to succumb to the dictatorial policies of a totalitarian state. Intelligence, not in an individual sense but in a social sense, shall provide the necessary man-made social authority needed at the present time. The process by which this authority is established is the technique of consensus, first a local and later a large scale consensus which binds the whole society to majority-approved action. The minority may dissent in voice but not in action when a consensus becomes the expression of the majority. The public schools possess the capabilities of directing this whole process of consensus, and after consensus has been attained, the public schools themselves obviously will be regulated in their activity by these majority decrees which, however, may change from time to time. The reconstructionists must by all means correct the key weaknesses of pragmatic indecision by outlining an unequivocal basis of authority for social action, for a realistic appraisal of our present needs shows that social order requires some definite kind of cultural authority.

Discipline, now becoming a problem in the schools, is not to be obtained by an "interest" appeal (progressive), nor by an authoritarian pedagogue (classical humanism) who assumes responsibility for the discipline of the group, but rather by group control itself. Discipline is formulated by the group, and it is imposed by the group. Majority-established discipline is neither soft not sentimental, but imposes stern requirements upon its members. Minorities must conform in action to group consensus, though they must always be guaranteed the privilege to voice dissent in public discussion. It is the conviction of the reconstructionist that no discipline is so effective in redirecting the straying individual as group discipline, and consequently there is no method so effective in establishing responsible action on the part of each individual in the group. In a sense, reconstructionist discipline is a force which *makes* the individual lose himself in order to find himself. Individual differences are played down at the beginning of the disciplinary process in order that corporately, at the end of the process, the individual is enhanced with a greater freedom by virtue of his membership in the group.

If a long range view is taken of the problem of responsibility, the position of the reconstructionist comes more clearly into focus as an up-to-date adjustment to the changing modes of thought and action in the world. In the case of the primitives the prevailing concept was a kind of "horde responsibility" where there were strict limits to individual choices. Western civilization stimulated individual competition, hence the irresistible swing toward individual action and individual responsibility. This was a great step forward over the primitive, but a stride toward a more complicated form of culture is the new concept of group responsibility, which is a kind of "sharing responsibility." At present this concept of responsibility is best expressed in small-group sharing, strongly recommended as an educational procedure. Eventually this concept will evolve itself into larger and larger areas of group planning. Planning becomes the key to the establishment of social responsibility. All persons share in planning and in the formation of group consensus, and this process psychologically identifies the individual with the group process, developing in him a sense of social responsibility. This is the basis for a remarkable amount of emphasis in recent educational theory on group dynamics, on the encouragement of more intercommunication, committee action, conferences, discussions. The more advanced theorists now talk about problem-centered groups which discuss social problems, analyze them, come to conclusions, and then act. "Social action" is one of the latest concepts of a substantial basis for an enduring democracy. If there is an evidence of individual responsibility in a collective society, it is simply the obligation of the individual to identify himself with the group process, involving himself in group discussion, by which consensus is obtained and programs for the general welfare are initiated. In that same sense, irresponsibility is conceived as the resistance of the individual will to share in the collective will. This is a modern conclusion not far afield from the earlier views of Rousseau when he argued that the general will of the society is identified with infallible right, forming the consensus of the group, and nothing should stand between the individual and his loyalty to this group consensus in a democratic regime.

The scaling up of the concept of responsibility to the social level places a new emphasis upon the problem of intergroup relationships, a situation which must become more and more a vital concern of education. Minority problems are actually majority problems, and they must be solved primarily on the group level. More intensive scientific research is required in the areas of intergroup relationships in order scientifically to establish clear-cut responsible group interaction. This challenge, in terms of social responsibilities, appeals particularly to the social psychologists, undoubtedly influenced by the Kurt Lewin school, who consider the issue of proper group relationships to be possibly the greatest contemporary problem of society.

At the base of this whole point of view, then, is the assumption that a twentieth century concept of responsibility and education's relation to it involves not the traditional or even the pragmatic approach, but a group approach to the problem. The modern environment, different from anything previously experienced, has engendered a recession in moral and rational progress. The traditional concepts of morality, couched in an individualistic framework, have now in a sense become propagators of individual irresponsibility, because the old order no longer applies to the new age and so tends to be divisive. The nature of modern society inevitably decrees more state control, emphasis on security, and the control of all phases of social activity. This collectivistic trend, so inevitable and inescapable, calls for one of two possible solutions: dictatorial control or democratic group planning. In fact, planning itself is inevitable, and for a people dedicated to the democratic way of life there must be a radical adjustment to the idea that planning and the democratic process are not at all exclusive to each other and that a negligent or an obstructive attitude toward social planning may weaken the democratic vitality of a society so that it succumbs to an autocratic form of totalitarianism.

In the face of a continuing social crisis, therefore, the reconstructionist insists on the educational utilization of every means to help young people learn "about the quality and quantity of what we want and how we get what we want."[5] The process of consensus, concerning what it is that the majority wants and how it is to be obtained, begins in earnest in the public schools with the lowest grades through the intensification of the group process, involving all manner of councils and committees for students, parents, service employees, citizens—everyone who in any way is directly or indirectly involved in public education. Teachers should reach for power and use it wisely in order to promote

5 Brameld, 541.

the process of consensus democratically. They should be strongly committed to the democratic ideal which insists that all forces tending toward class distinction should be controverted. On the part of teachers there should be an active resistance to every form of privilege, a responsiveness to the underprivileged, an exaltation of human labor, a devotion to equality among races, a supreme loyalty to the interests of the masses.

The teacher should be thoroughly grounded in modern psychological and sociological principles which are the basis for intelligent reconstruction. He should be concerned with the problem of group conflict, the principles of social psychology, anthropology, economics, political science, history. The teacher should deliberately center the school activities upon debatable social, political, and economic problems which currently are critical issues. Basic debatable questions should become prominent features of the educational curriculum. The continual critical review of the roles of the family, of religion, and of government is essentially important. These problems constitute the basis of learning, especially those social problems which block the goal-seeking society from reaching its national and international goals.

The practical educational problem heretofore posed for the pragmatists and the classical humanists is ideally constituted, it would seem, to show the reconstructionist approach in the best light. Surely there is no educational problem more basic to the thinking of the reconstructionists than that of intergroup relationships, in this case the harmonization of racial groups in the community.

The pragmatists attempt to solve this problem by means of an intelligent approach, and the classical humanists emphasize basically the means of reason and the law. In contrast, the reconstructionists suggest a new approach which would revise the concept of individual intelligence into the new idea of social intelligence, this social ability to be fostered by group dynamics, group consensus, group action.

The educational reconstructionist suggests at least three important approaches to the solution of this problem of responsible intergroup relationships in the community. The first point outlines the actual groundwork which is done in the schools of the community. The whole philosophy of the school program is revised in such a way that the emphasis is shifted from the "I" to the "we." This orientation starts at the lowest levels of education with a program of group interaction. Public school nurseries are sponsored in order to submit the child to the wholesome impact of socialization at a most impressionable age. Teachers and administrators forsake the roles of individual directors and leaders, and commit themselves to the task of fostering the group process. The total environment of the child is group oriented, from the bottom up. The administrative policies of the school, the faculty meetings, and teacher-pupil relationships are group oriented, wherein all persons associated with school life are given an increasing public share in decisions which in any way affect them. Social problems—in this case the race question—are directly faced and discussed; they are included as an integral part of the school curriculum. Education becomes a means for the group to think and feel its way toward community-accepted ends.

Group dynamics is the key to the reconstructionist curriculum and likewise the key to the particular problem now being considered. The teacher, even though he is not a sociological expert, can use relatively simple social techniques in order to bolster the group processes, such as the sociogram by means of which he can obtain a reasonably scientific picture of the group structure of his class, who are the key persons which the group holds in high regard, who are the group outcasts, the divisions of the group into cliques, and so on. This knowledge is invaluable to the instructor in intelligently promoting "in-group" growth, helping lone individuals learn to be a part of the group, and bringing closer together different small factions within the larger group. The teacher recognizes his secondary position in maintaining group morals personally and instead directs his energies toward the intensification of group togetherness, establishing a community spirit which automatically resolves many of the problems of discipline and motivation in learning. The more success the teacher has in establishing the group spirit and eliminating the lone eagle spirit in his class, the closer he comes to establishing a total milieu which is essential to the solution of the practical problem at hand.

A second phase of the educational reconstructionist's attack on the problem of racial relationships follows in the extension of the principles of group dynamics from the school to the community. This transition is quite reasonably possible because the school already has integrated basic community problems into the school curriculum. The actual process of group dynamics practised by the school in its administrative-teacher, administrative-employee, and administrative-teacher-pupil relationships has already involved the wider community, including elements of the minority groups, represented possibly by the janitors and other service employees. Since the curriculum is community oriented, it is a natural outcome that the school shall more and more integrate its activities with the community through its tours, projects, and investigations; through the use of community facilities and talents in the educational processes of the school; and through its community work programs. This ever widening group process sooner or later is bound to involve the direct attention of the students on the race problems of the community, and these problems will be faced not by some elite or intellectual group, but by many persons intimately concerned with the problem.

In the group discussions of these problems, public rather than private, the basic issues of sufficient nourishment, adequate dress, equal status, become prominent issues discussed by all types of persons in the school and eventually in the community. This kind of interplay of ideas, wherein the problems involving the minority groups are seen partially from the perspective of the minorities themselves, is bound to have a salutary effect upon the thinking of the whole community. Furthermore, the actual experience of such group dynamics involving all sections, cutting across caste and class lines, establishes a line of communication between various groups and classes which previously did not exist. The middle walls of partition are broken down, and men no longer think and feel and act in isolation. Prejudices are thereby softened, and the understanding becomes enlightened. Once the point is reached where there is a reasonable toleration of minority groups, the total community morale will be inestimably raised, and a really substantial foundation will be laid for mutual respect and co-operation between all groups. The whole process will be continually undergirded by participation, the sharing in responsible group decisions, the magnification of the sense of belonging, and the increase of mutual appreciation which comes through co-operative activity. The basic reconstructionist principles involved in this solution to the problem are first, that communication is basic; second, that learning is most effective through group dynamics and that here is discovered the basis of social consensus; third, that the wider and wider effect of group dynamics establishes a kind of super ego which includes all kinds of peoples and all classes, and by this means the individual is group oriented; and fourth, that this whole procedure is public, open, always subject to community examination.

And finally, the educational reconstructionist theorist is concerned with the processes of group dynamics not only to solve immediate problems but to institute a drive systematically to reduce the intensity of the individualistic competitive spirit. The educational reconstructionist hopes to supplant the spirit of individualism with the ritual of co-operation as it is experienced in the group processes. When this goal is accomplished, men will be freed for higher levels of responsibility so that they may creatively engage in productive activities for the welfare of all mankind, so that they may work unhampered by the traditional influences of individualism and selfish competition.

The educational reconstructionist is convinced that the total effect of the group processes in a community will supply the clearly demarcated patterns for "social-self-realization." These group processes give the individual in the community that sense of stability which socially supports him for responsible action. Group participation leads to group orientation in man's thinking and in his responses. The purposes of the community become more clear to him and consequently more challenging, calling for his co-operation and dedication. Always there is in operation in the group processes the psychological principle that sharing in group *decisions* automatically dignifies the sharing in group *responsibilities*. The continuing identification of the individual with the group through group processes effectively lessens the irresponsible actions of the egoist in isolation, and one's egoistic tendencies are thus largely offset by the intellectual power which is generated through participation in group decisions and actions. The new world is a collective world, and it requires a sound, scientific emphasis of the group processes in order to insure the development of a collective responsibility, the only ideal force which insures a reasonable chance for the survival of a twentieth century democratic society.

PART FOUR

Education, the Community, and Christian Faith

CHAPTER TEN

Education, the State, and Christian Faith

Today the proper relationship of Christian faith to public education is a serious problem. It is reasonably safe to say that the educational history of the United States is quite unintelligible apart from Christian faith. Christian influence is deeply felt not only by contemporary leaders in education, progressivists and classical humanists, but even by educational reconstructionists who admit certain Christian ethical forms pervading their otherwise non-Christian educational faith.

Although it is relatively simple to argue the vital historical relationship between Christian faith and public education, it seems extremely difficult to analyze this relationship. Education is complicated by its divergent philosophies, and Christendom is beset with its manifold variations of faith. These deviations in both areas create many tensions: philosophy against philosophy, faith against faith, and philosophy against faith.

Early American education was without doubt predominantly a Protestant Christian enterprise. A vigorous Reformation faith decreed that all men are individually accountable to a sovereign God; all men, therefore, ought to be taught to read the Bible in order to fulfill their theological responsibilities. So believed the early Puritans of New England who are credited with a major contribution to the religious foundations of the public school in America.

The same faith which emphasized strongly the responsibility of every man to God also insisted that all men are basically unreliable when they are tempted with power. When the problem of government was faced, it was decided that power and authority ought to be placed in the hands of many. A constitution was written which provided checks and balances to counteract the ever present human failing to misuse state power. By virtue of this lively Protestant faith in the sovereignty of God and man's obligation to Him, along with a parallel distrust in the natural perfectibility of man, early America organized a unique kind of education and launched a remarkable governmental experiment in the new world. Both the new education and the new state proceeded "under God," and both proclaimed that "in God we trust."

Because early Protestantism in America took its faith seriously both for the individual and for the community, it was vulnerable to schism, a common weakness in groups who take faith seriously. The Protestant insistence that every man is his own priest before God supported a fresh and vital form of individualism. Yet the wholesome diversity which this doctrine inspired also made possible a trend toward unwholesome fragmentation. Some of the strength of Protestantism was transformed to weakness when various groups seemingly misunderstood and misused their Christian liberties. Eventually a proliferation of the sects and a subsequent intensity of conflict among them, often about peripheral matters, necessitated the formulation of new laws to separate religious conflict from public education. And in the days of Horace Mann it was decided that no religious sectarian instruction must be given in the public schools and that public funds must not be granted to sectarian schools.

During this era the strife between sectarian groups was apparently serious enough to obscure the central core of theological faith which was yet common ground for the contending sects. Dissension about lesser religious problems occupied the center of the stage to the extent that the central theological faith which provided the infinitely valuable framework for both school and state was not treasured properly, but was seemingly taken for granted.

Our twentieth century historical perspective shows how much important headway nontheological world views had already gained by the middle of the nineteenth century. While the common Christian faith of the nation was being taken for granted, the minds of the educated were already excited by novel and fascinating naturalistic faiths: organic evolution, the possibilities of the scientific method, the dream of progress. Faith in reason and in nature was subtly displacing the Reformation concept of faith in God.

At the beginning of the twentieth century, educational philosophers ambitiously viewed the prospect of creating the good life by means of newly discovered knowledge—physical, biological, psychological, sociological. John Dewey led the way in outlining a philosophy which turned its face against traditional absolutes and placed its confidence in scientifically established criteria based upon experience. The scientific method was expected to revolutionize moral knowledge in the same way that it was already transforming knowledge of the physical world. But the educational flowering of this secular faith was cut short by two disastrous world wars and a great depression.

As early as 1930 educators were seriously reconsidering their ebullient secular optimism. The forward movement of secular programs was being distracted by the harsh realities of war and want. Unexpected pressures upon education revealed latent weaknesses stemming from a lack of common faith. Confusion and uncertainty generated many competing faiths, each attempting to supply the answers to education's new problems. Now educators began to talk more seriously, with some nostalgia it seemed, about the earlier common theological faith which effectively provided an integrative framework for education. But it was evident that powerful secular faiths had seriously weakened the original foundations. Many educators were coming to the conclusion that a common faith ought to be restored to education, but there was little agreement about what that faith should be. The pragmatists and the reconstructionists believing in a dynamic novel universe argued that we needed a new faith for a new age. The classical humanists said that education had forsaken the classical emphasis on reason and that education restored to the life of reason would dispel the confusion. And a resurging Christian faith with its two outstanding traditional forms, Roman Catholicism and Reformation faith, insisted that education's dilemma could be traced to its separation from Christian faith or at least to the weakening of Christian foundations.

Today secularism in education represented by pragmatic and reconstructionist views presents democracy as the new faith which best supports a dynamic and diversified educational program. As theological faith fulfilled the needs of an earlier age, so democracy as a new faith can fulfill the needs of the present age. As theological foundations once commonly supported both education and the state, so a secular democratic faith can now provide the foundation for modern education and the modern state. The new faith carries great potentiality because it is nontheological and therefore nonsectarian. Its purposes relate themselves to all of the people. The democratic faith considers the principle of the separation of church and state extremely important, for dogmatic supernaturalisms tend to be divisive and they ought to be detained outside the high wall of separation to prevent them from impeding the development of this common faith.

The creed of this secular democratic faith is centered in the ideals of human dignity, equality, and freedom. Final authority rests in the democratic state which derives its authority from the people. In times of national and international crisis it may be necessary for the state to assume more direct control of the educative processes in order to insure the democratization of its citizenry, in order to support more effectively the democratic processes of sharing and group participation so that the young may be better grounded in responsible democratic citizenship.

The Roman Catholic Church with its separative practices in contemporary American education represents a formidable threat to this secular democratic faith. The hope of a common democratic faith for all of the people is difficult to achieve indeed when a gigantic organization of some 29,000,000 souls officially withdraws its young from public education and proposes to educate them in separate schools where practicable and to found them in a religious faith which is admittedly thoroughly opposed to the powerful nontheological faiths which now permeate public education.

The Roman Catholic Church was a small minority group in early America. During the past hundred years, however, it has added to its rolls a multitude of Catholic immigrants who came to the United States from Europe. In addition it has undergone a modern spiritual renaissance, due partially at least to an unwavering adherence to its faith in this present age of uncertainty. These developments have contributed substantially to the establishment in America of a powerful ecclesiastical organization which traditionally carries with it a determined and unapologetic philosophy of education.

The parents rather than the state, insists the Roman Catholic Church, are primarily responsible for the education of their children. It is the parents who are accountable to God through the church for administering the right kind of education. Since parents cannot fulfill this obligation individually (education is a social function), the church considers it necessary to provide the right kind of education for the children of believers. Actually education is not Christian unless it is presided over by the Christian ecclesia—

which of course is exclusively the Roman Catholic Church. And "there can be no ideally perfect education which is not Christian education."[1]

Long experience has shown that the Roman Catholic Church and the family are best qualified to promote the education of children. The church therefore considers it justifiable to agitate politically, if necessary, to fulfill its educational purposes for the young. The idea of the separation of church from school cannot be tolerated, because the church is the spiritual guardian of education. It is necessary to the state as well as to the church that children learn the meaning of personal and community responsibility under the spiritual direction of God's chosen organization. The state has its area of temporal authority, but the church uncompromisingly claims the primary authority in moral and spiritual matters. And many of the most profound moral and spiritual responsibilities are unquestionably involved in the educative processes.

This problem of authority points to the heart of the dilemma for education, because it not only involves a controversial relationship between Christian faith and secular faiths, but also indicates a basic cleavage at the center of Christendom itself.

For the Neo-Thomist, God the Creator is absolutely sovereign. And God is the creator and sustainer of natural law. Man learns about God and about truth through two important channels: first, through the discovery of natural law, and second, by divine revelation through the Roman Catholic Church. Man through the proper development of his reason can discover authoritative truth by learning about God's laws which sustain His creation, and through the church the believer receives higher truth which is revealed by God. Rationally discovered truth and revealed truth coming from the same source must always support one an-

1 Encyclical letter of Pope Pius XI on "Christian Education of Youth."

other. Moral and spiritual persons by means of right reason and divine enlightenment are vested with unquestionable authority because they can speak the truth. There is a hierarchy of authority, however, in accordance with the level in which truth is discovered. The authority of rationally discovered truth is not equal to authority based upon revealed truth (which is the primary basis for the authority of the church). Men by reason can discover truth which supports their temporal authorities, but men by faith through the church learn the highest truth which carries with it the highest authority. The highest ability to speak the truth involves a parallel highest responsibility to command with authority.

Obviously this view of authority and truth evokes a violent reaction from nontheological secular democratic faiths which stand adamant against these claims of absolute authority, and education is the critical area where these faiths meet head on. The Roman Catholic Church cannot possibly subscribe in principle to an autonomous secular arrangement where the state or the individual can proceed on the basis that they are free of the church's higher authority. And modern secular democratic faith on the other hand cannot brook the proposition that any organization which is only a part of the whole can authoritatively command the whole in the name of God. The democratic equalitarian view insists that authority must reside in all persons concerned with any decision which carries authority with it. In the final analysis the people are sovereign. Authority is essentially internal, stemming from the group or the situation, rather than external, flowing from a power which stands above the situation.

Jacques Maritain, possibly the most distinguished of Catholic philosophers commonly known to American readers, presents a closely reasoned Catholic analysis of the question of church and state relationships. This noted philosopher first makes a serious point of distinguishing the state from what he calls the "body politic."[2] The body politic is the whole body of citizens of a nation. This body sustains within its life the whole gamut of cultural activity: thousands of different combinations of citizens centering upon a varied multitude of interests. The state, in contrast to the body politic, is the topmost part of the whole body of people, the hood of the people which protects and nourishes their cultural activities. The varied activity of the body politic is the work of reason extending upward, while the work of the state is reason (manifested through its works of justice) working downward. The state umpires and coerces, if necessary, and it has the power to fulfill these assignments, but the direct source of its power is the people. The state sponsors justice, but the state ought not to participate in, or become a part of, the cultural enterprises which take place within the body politic. As the referee does not play in the actual game, the state ought not actually to participate in the cultural activities of the people.

The authority of the state—and this is basic—is not ultimately sovereign authority. The government possesses power to rule, but the government must not claim ultimate authority for itself. The state is immediately answerable to the people and ultimately answerable to God who is sovereign over all. And the organization on earth which is the chosen representative of the eternal sovereign God is the Roman Catholic Church. The state is answerable temporally to the people and eternally to God.

If this be the position of the state, it seems obvious that education ought not to be subject, in its cultural and spiritual aspects, to the unequivocal authority of the state, nor ought education to be the function of the state, for education is not the legitimate business of the state any more than playing the game is the legitimate function of the umpire.

[2] In the discussions which follow, Jacques Maritain's book, *Man and the State,* is heavily drawn upon for outlining the Roman Catholic viewpoint.

Education is a cultural activity which ought to be under the jurisdiction of an authority higher than the state, and this higher authority is the Roman Catholic Church. The state by all means ought to co-operate with education and to support education, but the actual functioning of education is a family commitment, and the extension of this family responsibility is a church assignment. Just as the state ought to encourage all of the cultural activities of the body politic, it ought also to encourage and support education, but the state ought to acknowledge the higher authority of the church in spiritually guiding the educational process.

Since the modern state is more and more discovering that its own vitality is drawn from the spiritual strength which the church gives to the body politic (this is the Roman Catholic position), it ought to be particularly attentive to the work of Christian agencies in the realm of education. A nation which realizes that its beginnings and its prosperity are inseparable from Christian faith cannot afford to remain neutral about supporting the source of its strength. The church has the spiritual resources for solving the problem of developing responsible citizens. It is the urgent business of the state to support the organization which knows through its godly wisdom the manner and the means of best carrying out this educational assignment.

This position of the church in reference to authority in education is obviously unacceptable to the secular forces which control public education today. But this same question also creates a formidable barrier between Roman Catholic faith and Reformation Christian faith.

Martin Luther revived the New Testament implications of man's direct responsibility to God and the infinitely personal nature of man's relationship, by faith, to his Creator. Man's salvation is a personal matter, and nothing ought to come between him and God. Salvation involves an intensely active personal response to God and not only a passive acceptance of the dictates of the church. Salvation involves a meeting of persons: man meeting God; God discovering Himself to man. The person himself is in one sense an ultimate, and his personal relationship to God (not to the church) is the ultimate basis for his humanity and his salvation. The frightening aspect of every man's existence is that he can personally say yes or no to God his Creator. And this interpretation of man's existence involves a radical understanding of the nature of responsibility. With the Thomist view the church assumes considerable responsibility for man's salvation. The church makes many of the hard decisions, and its members accept the church's authority about these decisions. With the Reformation view a fuller weight of responsibility falls upon every individual who has reached the age of discretion.

According to the Reformers the emphasis upon the sovereignty of God is not primarily an organizational matter but a personal matter. The Schoolmen under the guise of ecclesiastical authority actually tended to draw a veil over the minds of men. Faith does not consist of placing trust in the authority of the church, but of personal knowledge. And men ought never to place their final confidence in divine teachers so called, because it is obvious, as Calvin observed, that "some portion of unbelief is always mixed with faith in every Christian." Christians, even though they are leaders in the household of faith, are yet sinners, and they cannot say that they possess the whole truth unmixed with error. To claim that the church, though made up of sinful and deficient men, is at the same time the body of Christ and therefore sinless as a community which functions officially in the name of Christ, does not take into account the radical nature of personal human sinfulness and the communal solidarity of sin as it is seen from the Reformation point of view. Because men even at their best are sinful, final authority simply cannot be centered in any group or organization, even though it claims to represent God on earth.

But history well shows that this Protestant revolt against the authority of the Roman Catholic Church has created some difficult problems for modern society. Protestantism has splintered into a confusing array of individualistic groups in the ecclesiastical realm, and in the world at large, men have perverted this Protestant revolt to mean that everyone could do as he pleased to satisfy his lust for unbridled freedom. The discipline and the authority which human beings seem desperately to need for their community life has been woefully dissipated in this modern age, and every man tends to do what is right in his own eyes. God was sovereign for the Reformers first of all in a personal sense, but the God of the Reformers has too often been personally discarded. And today pragmatism, Protestantism's illegitimate offspring, has virtually eliminated the sovereign God from its field of interest, and the disintegrative results are only too apparent in public education. Modern education in the name of the modern disciplines of psychology and sociology has sponsored a spirit of revolt against all kinds of traditional authorities, not the least of which is the God of the Bible.

The essential disagreement between Roman Catholic faith and Reformation faith about the question of church authority seems irreconcilable for the time being. The argument of the Catholic Church is strengthened by Protestantism's weaknesses resulting from an absence of a strong central integrative authority. The argument for the Protestant concept of authority is strengthened by the obvious misuses of authority which are to be observed in any highly centralized organization. Those persons or organizations who believe they unquestionably possess the truth and the authority which attaches to this truth are inevitably tempted with the sin of pride, which is the greatest undoer of all.

The strength of the Reformation position lies in its recognition of the radical nature of human sinfulness and in its assumption that the truth is not necessarily to be dispensed by him who claims a special rational talent or a special position in the ecclesiastical hierarchy, and not by the man who revolts against all forms of authority, but by the person who is genuinely humble in the presence of truth. Select men do not apprehend the deepest truth by virtue of their rational discipline or by virtue of the organization to which they belong, but by Christian faith, the fruit of which, among other things, is humility.

But this kind of relationship to truth involves a paradox: If one does not make an aggressive claim for possessing the truth, how can he act effectively with the truth which he possesses? What does humility have to offer in claiming the community for the good life? For one thing the administration of justice demands power and force on occasion. Reformation faith without question acknowledges the work of the state and need for power to support this work. The distinction comes in considering what basically is the work of the church in contrast to the work of the state. The work of the state with its external power and authority ought to be based upon reason as far as possible, but the concern of the church with deeper faith involves a relationship of humility to the body politic primarily, and not of force. The state ought to be related to education impersonally and forcefully insofar as the externals of education are concerned. But the church ought to be related to education in the realm of deeper truth, the fruits of which are faith and peace and gentleness. The power and the authority which attaches to the concern with personal truth ought to be a permeative spiritual power and not an organizational external authority. The church ought to command by its humility and not by its organizational might.

But the need for organizational influence cannot be minimized in the face of evil even in the best of societies. Reformation faith supports the concept of the state and its power as arbiter even over the church because the sinful nature of the community requires this authoritative control. The state rather than the church is the final arbiter where coercion and power are necessary, because the church ought not to be engaged primarily in the business of maintaining moral standards by force. Of course from a practical view a certain amount of organization is necessary in the church. To speak of permeative spiritual influence by the church tends to be an idealistic play on words in the light of the sinful nature of the church itself. Organization in the church and the authority which attaches to it can seemingly be justified because the church, like any other social group, is composed of sinful human beings. Now if the community in general requires organizational pressures and influences because of its moral and spiritual weaknesses, is it not also practical to assume that the church must deal organizationally with some of the spiritual weaknesses within itself and also with the cultural areas in the community for which it considers itself responsible? If this argument be valid—and the Roman Catholic Church once again demonstrates its practical understanding of what ought to be the relationship of church to cultural activities, particularly education—then historical Protestantism appears comparatively prostrate before the modern dilemma of its relationship to public education. Reformation faith is still generally committed to the principle of separation of church organizations from public education, and therefore it seems to have little means of practically supporting its own convictions about what ought to transpire in education in order to bring about a godly reorientation.

Before giving a final consideration to this whole problem of Reformation and Catholic faiths and their relationships to public education, it seems important to digress for one chapter at least to review the similarities and divergences of Reformation and Thomistic concepts of the nature of man. An outline of Reformation and Catholic anthropologies ought to provide a useful background for any serious attempt to discover practical means of lessening the tension within the Christian household of faith in order to strengthen the over-all Christian commitment to the restoration of a godly faith to the educational work of the community.

CHAPTER ELEVEN

Reformation and Thomistic Concepts
of the Nature of Man

THOMISM and Reformation faiths seem to stand side by side in their fundamental opposition to secular concepts of the nature of man. Yet there are serious differences of view between these two Christian outlooks which in some respects lead to widely separated positions in theology and in education. To trace the lines of agreement and divergence, however, is a difficult undertaking. Hebrew, Christian, Greek, and modern secular outlooks contribute to an interweaving of theological and philosophical themes which seem far beyond the comprehension of this review.

It is important to preface a study in contrasts with a brief review of similarities in the Catholic and Reformation versions of faith which constitute presuppositions for a Christian interpretation of the nature of man. As the sects in the nineteenth century erred in not being mindful of an important area of common agreement, there seems today a comparable danger that the two dominant streams of Christendom in America may obscure areas of faith common to both. Basic areas of agreement in Christian faith are infinitely important as foundations for the solution of difficult current educational problems, and they ought to provide a basis for working at these problems with genuine hope. In some respects, for example, conservative Protestantism seems to stand closer to the center of Catholic faith than it does to the more liberal and sometimes radical expressions of modern Protestantism. Possibly Neo-Reformation faith and Neo-Thomism as they turn back more and more to their original sources for refreshment and revival will discover that their paths at first were not far apart. The clashes on the periphery of faith, magnified by the centuries, may have cast a confusing haze over common beginnings. Divergent lines near their point of origin are close, even though their extension into space leaves them eventually far apart.

Serious consideration ought to be given, for example, to the common faith in the God of the Bible, the sovereign God who created the world out of nothing and who momentarily sustains this whole created universe and all who are in it. Essential agreement is also evident about the doctrine that man stands in personal relationship to his Creator, that man was first created good and that now he suffers from defect and corruption. In the final analysis both outlooks agree that faith stands above reason, and both agree that the state is for man and not man for the state. Both the Thomist and the Reformation faiths ascribe to the basic doctrines of the Apostle's Creed; both show a high respect for Augustine, one of the greatest of the early church fathers.

Actually the leading figures of the Reformation were hesitant about a radical break with the mother church. And even after this seemingly inevitable step had been taken, the Reformation leaders outlined a Reformed pattern which was in many respects essentially Catholic. For this reason some liberal Protestant theologians today are inclined to label the revival of Reformation faith as a revival of Catholic Protestantism.

Yet in the face of all of these arguments for common ground, it must be recognized that theological divergences in the earlier centuries, extended through time, have created a wide gulf between the present positions of these theological faiths. And the wideness of this gulf substantially contributes to the woes of current education in America. It would seem that the best way to understand these critical aberrations is to trace at least summarily a few of the differences of interpretation about man's nature. As one Catholic philosopher has said, the purposes of education hinge upon the question of the "precise nature of the educand." Educational philosophers of all descriptions seem inclined to agree with this pronouncement.

The Christian problem of how to describe man's nature leads all the way back to a key statement in Genesis: "And God said, Let us make man in our image, after our likeness."[1] At first glance it seems fantastic to think that this short sentence formulated in ancient times should have an all-important relationship to twentieth century problems in American public education. Nevertheless, when that early writer of Scripture added the complementary phrase "after our likeness," he set in motion the formulation of a theological pattern for the whole Roman Catholic Church during the past millenium. And this theological pattern is crucial to American education today.

In order to understand why this phrase "after our likeness" is so important, we must refer to the significant influence of ancient Greek philosophy on early Christian faith. It is true that some of the early church fathers condemned pagan philosophies, but other influential theologians believed the ideas of the Greeks important enough to be used in the systematic formulation of Christian faith. Irenaeus in the third century worked out a synthesis between philosophy and Christian theology which was a forerunner of the eventual magnificent synthesis of Thomas Aquinas. This synthesis, insofar as an understanding of man's nature is concerned, deals in a supremely important fashion with the Genesis statement that God created man in His own *image* and after His *likeness*. The image of God in man, said Irenaeus, and Aquinas later, is man's reason. This is a conclusion which harmonizes particularly with the Greek view. And the *likeness* of God in man, said the theologians, is man's

[1] Genesis 1:26.

original supernature, given him by God in order that man could enjoy personal fellowship with the Creator. This is a conclusion drawn from Christian faith, and of course it is revealed wisdom which stands above philosophical knowledge. The Greeks through their natural philosophical capacities did an amazing piece of work in discovering by reason the idea of Infinite Reason. This discovery was the basis of the Greek understanding of the humanity of man. Man infused by the divine Reason becomes human and infinitely distinctive from the lower creatures. Yet the Greeks could not discover by reason the personal nature of God. This knowledge was made known to man by God through revelation. God is not only Infinite Reason but God the Father. This is the message of the church. Man is not only made in the *image* of God (what the Greeks discovered), but man is also made in the *likeness* of God (what was revealed to the church). Man is really a two-storied being. His natural being is dignified by reason, and his supernatural being is a special human capacity to enjoy personal fellowship with God the Creator. The *image* denotes a kind of rational substance which makes man human and different from the other creatures. The *likeness* indicates a special capacity for relationship with God.

This interpretation of man in the ancient and medieval church was not by any means the only theological position. Many of the earlier theologians, including Augustine, placed reason in a much less favorable light and preferred a Gospel personalism unconditioned by Greek rationalism. We believe in order to know, said Augustine. But the thirteenth century saw a shift away from Augustinian influence and an increasing infusion of Christian theology with Aristotelian ideas. At this point Thomas Aquinas with his respect for Aristotle lifted reason to a more favorable status in the church. Rather than categorically insisting that we must believe in order to know, Aquinas made a distinction between the realm of knowing by reason and the realm of knowing by faith. The natural man created in the image of God is gifted with the unique capacity to reason and thereby to order the institutions of temporal society. To this extent reason is supremely important. Yet the life of man is more than a temporal consideration. Life is eternal, and the wisdom which man needs to contemplate the eternal aspects of his existence comes through Christian faith. Since the eternal life stands above the temporal life, faith obviously stands above reason. But this distinction by no means degrades the value of reason. Reason is good because reasoning is a human capacity made possible by the "image" of God in man.

This Thomistic interpretation of the Genesis account is not only significant for the place it gives reason in the Christian understanding of the nature of man, but also for the remarkable fashion by which it rationalizes the dogma of original sin. Both the Reformation and Catholic faiths believe that God created man without sin. Since all mankind is now under sin, it seems necessary to conclude that man has suffered a fall. Yet societies of men apart from Christian faith often show evidences of human goodness and refinement. The problem is how to account for this fact and still to recognize the evidences of a fall. The Catholic synthesis provides a neat answer for this question. Man created in the *image* of God possesses the capacity to reason. The rational substance which constitutes man's image of God humanizes all men, even though all men are fallen. The fall of man relates therefore not to the *image* but to the *likeness* of God in man. As a result of original sin man lost this special fellowship with God. Man was deprived of his supernature, but man was not deprived of the "image" of God, his reason. Now the restoration of the supernature (the "likeness") is the work of God through the church, and there is no human means by which this restoration can be effected. The church alone mediates this work of grace.

There is enough similarity between the Greek idea of

evil and the medieval idea of evil to add further significance to the Thomistic synthesis of Greek philosophy and Christian theology. In both cases there is a primary emphasis upon the idea of incompleteness. For the Greeks evil is often explained in terms of the potential failing of actuality. Evil stems from the incomplete nature. The Thomistic Christian concept of original sin also suggests that man's sinful state derives from his incompleteness resulting from the loss of his supernature. Original sin is not associated with something positive in man, but rather with his deprived condition. Aquinas taught that being is convertible with truth and goodness, which seems to imply that the false and the bad are in some manner associated with a lesser or greater degree of nonbeing. With this kind of teaching surely Aristotle would not be inclined to disagree.[2]

When the Reformation took place in the sixteenth century, it seems that an outstanding factor in this upheaval was the questionable impact of Greek philosophy in the church. The Reformation in one respect was a powerful revolt against certain unfortunate rationalized accessories of this great ecclesiastical organization. The Reformers felt a need for the church to return to the fundamentals of the Bible itself. In the Reformation movement the confluence of Christian theology and Greek philosophy was seriously disrupted. And the challenge was sharp against the traditional Catholic concept of the nature of man, against the idea that man was originally created as a two-storied being with a good rational being (image) which man still possessed and a supernatural likeness which man had lost.

Martin Luther was the leader in this new evaluation of the Catholic understanding of man's nature. Luther argued that the early Genesis statement about *image* and *likeness* was simply an example of the Hebrew literary habit of em-

---

[2] Emil Brunner's book *Man in Revolt* discusses in detail this whole question of Christian anthropology.

phasis. Image and likeness, said Luther, refer to the same thing. The idea of a double level arrangement of man's nature is an artificial dualism. Man is a single being who responds with his whole heart to his Creator and to other persons.

In terms of twentieth century knowledge, the Neo-Reformation theologians have suggested that the significance of man's humanity is his "relationship" to God. Man is not human in the medieval sense by virtue of a rational substance which exists in his being, but rather because the whole man is in distinctive *relationship* to God. God created man in His own image, which is to say that man is a person. But the Neo-Reformation theologians mean something different from the Scholastics when they use the term "person." The medieval definition by Boethius says: "Person is an individual substance of a rational nature."[3] By contrast the theologians of the Reformation revival speak of the concept of the person as the most profound of all realities and of the essential significance of personal existence as *relationship* and not *rational substance*. Reason is one of the capacities of a person, but not that which determines the person. The person is the subject, and the only way man can know the subject is through personal relationship—and this is a reality beyond the power of reason alone to grasp. The origin of the human person is deep in the heart of the eternal Person. The origin of the person is a divine mystery, and the closest man can describe it is to say that the creation of man is an act of divine love. The true relationship between persons is love. Love is the highest expression of a person. This kind of personal relationship is suprarational. God makes Himself known to man through His divine love. Personal relationship involves the whole man, and this means his reason, his will, his feelings, responding as a unity. Man responds to the eternal Person with his whole heart by faith.

3 Runes (ed.), *The Dictionary of Philosophy,* 229.

Faith like love is the profound expression of the whole man toward another person.

This Reformation concept of the person and his relationship to God led to an entirely different kind of interpretation of the fall of man. As mentioned earlier, the Thomistic view suggests that the fall of man consisted in the deprivation of his supernature, but that man retained his rational being (which was good) , and this accounted for his humanity even after his fall. Since the Reformer believed that man as a whole is related to God the Creator, the idea of the fall of man indicated that the whole man had fallen. And this revolutionary concept meant that man's reason too had fallen. For the Reformers the whole man becomes perverted and affected by his fall; for the Catholic position only the supernature is radically affected. The distinction of utmost significance at this point is that for the Thomist the fall means that man is deprived. For the Reformer the fall means that man is depraved. The Reformation leaders taught that man's reason, will, and feelings—all that is man— are tainted by sin and therefore are basically untrustworthy.

This radical Reformation view of man's fall created a serious problem for Protestant theology. If all of man's nature is perverted, how could the refined cultures and the natural good in pagan and heathen civilizations be explained? The Catholic view said the answer is to be found in reason, a substance in man existing unimpaired by original sin. Neo-Reformation theologians today try to answer this question by teaching that the humanity which natural man still possesses must also be explained in terms of relationship rather than as rational substance. Even though every man is a sinner, every man is still related to God. The relationship is there; it is not good, but a bad relationship is still a relationship. God by His infinite power who made the world out of nothing continues in His infinite love to sustain every man. Even more, though man is a sinner, he remains a creation in the image of God. The inhumanity

which man demonstrates comes not from defect or deprivation but from a positively bad relationship to the Creator.
Perfect humanity stems not from perfect reason but from
perfect relationship to the Creator. Perfect relationship is
responsive relationship. Bad relationships between man and
God, or man and man, are irresponsible relationships. The
problem of responsibility is personal, suprarational, theological. The exercise of reason is an integral part of responsible
relationships between persons, but the Greek idea of putting
reason on a pedestal is unacceptable to Reformation faith,
whether this idea be purely classical humanism or medieval
Christianity.

The Roman Catholic belief that human nature is deprived
but not depraved and that through the church human nature
is restored by grace gives a clearer understanding for divergent views about truth and authority. Because reason in
man remains intact in principle at least, reason can discover
truth which is certain, according to the Thomist view. Reason can proceed from self-evident truth to general principles
which are genuinely authoritative. This faith in the authority of reason was the hope of the classic Greek philosophers in refuting the relativism of their time. Today Catholic
philosophers share the confidence of the classical humanists
in authoritative truth as discovered in natural law. But in
addition the church relies upon another source of authoritative truth divinely revealed. Since the church is God's
chosen vehicle for the dissemination of spiritual truth, the
church is infallible when it speaks the truth in the name of
God. The Roman Catholic Church has combined the unquestionable authority of reason with its divine commission
to speak with unquestioned spiritual authority. With this
kind of command of the truth the church has the inalienable
right to speak with authority and to insist upon obedience
to its truth. And possession of this kind of truth presupposes
the right to command.

Reformation faith cannot subscribe to this Thomistic concept of truth and authority, and the ground, it seems, for this Reformation dissent is the Protestant dogma that human nature is not only "deprived" but "depraved." In saying man is depraved, the Reformers did not mean that human nature is totally bad, but rather that no part of human nature is free from the perverting influences of sin. The whole man is affected by sin. This conclusion placed the Reformers in sharp opposition to Thomistic optimism about reason, because reason too, according to Reformation faith, is tainted with sin. The significance of man's humanity lies in the responsive relationship of the whole man to God. By the same token the significance of the depravity of the whole man lies in the perverted relationship of the whole person to God. This idea leads to the Reformation conclusion that all men are sinners to the extent that they cannot lay claim to unquestionable truth and unquestionable authority. It is true that man has much good in him, but evil always overcomes the good regardless of the level of personal ethics or the refinement of the culture or the plane of rational development. There is no solid foundation within the nature of man upon which to found claims of having the truth. Reason, if it be man's only hope for working out his own salvation, claims illustrious progress for itself, but in the end reason succumbs to a sin which is the most terrible of all—pride. Therefore absolute authority cannot be vested in any organization or person, and therefore the only hope for a temperate and balanced authority lies in the people. But they must be good people. Hence the Reformation bent toward public education which gave every person the means to become a good person, a good citizen.

These concepts about man's capacity to fulfill himself show an interesting progression as one traces them from Greek classical humanism to the synthesis of Aquinas and finally to Reformation faith. In the Greek sense man possesses the potential for his fulfillment, and this fulfillment is effected through the work of reason. Thus education is a basic theme in the whole Greek culture because it is the process of actualizing man's potential, uniting him to God, attuning man with the Infinite, so to speak. But Thomas Aquinas refutes the idea that man can save himself by reason alone. Salvation comes through the church as it brings about the restoration of the deprived part of man's nature through the church's word of truth and the sacraments. Once grace has been added to natural reason, man has acquired the capacity to work out his salvation in history. In contrast to these views the Reformers took the radical position that salvation is acquired by the grace of God alone, through faith. Salvation is completely a gift, and one cannot work at it as do the Catholics, after receiving God's grace through the church, or as do those of secular faith who believe that reason alone is enough. Furthermore, the Reformers insisted that the grace of God did not give man the capacity to dispense the truth. Even after a man was regenerated by God through faith, he was still a sinner and subject to error. When any man tries authoritatively to outline the truth, he colors it with his own sinfulness. The Neo-Reformation theologians therefore insist that a Protestant view of truth and authority must emphasize a dominant theme of humility. No person, saved or unsaved, can claim to be the authoritative possessor and dispenser of truth. This pretension is the subtlest of errors.

This Reformation conclusion about truth and authority undoubtedly has its serious drawbacks. Neo-Reformation faith is forced to outline for itself a kind of complicated dialectical explanation about these matters. There can be no forceful and direct claim to certainty and authority on the one hand, and yet on the other hand, Reformation faith too must speak of truth with certainty and authority. This problem makes it necessary for theologians like Niebuhr to talk about "having and not having the truth." And of course once the Protestant position moves away from the Catholic assumption of an unequivocal claim to spiritual truth and authority, its defence against secular relativism becomes a hazardous proposition. Pragmatism seems to be a notable modern example of a reconstructed Protestantism made possible through the liberalization of ideas about God and the authority of the Bible. In fact, at this point we can see the progression carrying through from one extreme to the other. The classical humanists and the Thomists say that the truth is the truth and we have it. Neo-Reformation theologians usually claim that the truth is reliable and unchanging but because we are sinful men we cannot say that we have it; we can only say "we have it and we don't have it." The pragmatists, retaining a Protestant form but eliminating God, arrive at the extreme position of assuming that since we cannot know whether God really exists, we can only judge for practical purposes that all truth is relative. Therefore, say the pragmatists, no one has the truth, because apparently truth does not exist absolutely in the first place.

The classical humanists insist that man infused with the divine Reason can perceive what are the eternal principles to be followed in the perfection of his nature, and it follows that man's education can be definitely outlined and organized in the light of his rational nature. The Thomists concur, but they add to the authority of reason the authority of the church, which is the authority of God, and by the authority of the church they point out that the end of man is not for this temporal life alone, but for divine fellowship with God the Father. And the Catholic Church, concerned not only with the good life for this world but for the world to come, must exercise prior authority in the supervision of the educational process so that education not only takes into account a rational development of the learner in preparation for temporal life, but the spiritual development also in preparation for eternal life.

The Reformation faith, by contrast, with its radical doctrine of the sinfulness of all men (and of the whole man) cannot logically set itself up as a final authority in the affairs of this temporal life. Reformation faith is opposed to centering unquestioned authority in any man or any human organization, the Roman Catholic Church notwithstanding. The problem of sin precludes the assumption that even the church can speak with divine and unquestioned authority in human affairs, including education. The concept of personal responsibility in the divine-human encounter suggests that no man or organization can speak with final authority about, or step between, this infinitely serious relationship. Dictatorial men or dictatorial organizations, no matter how benign or necessary the form of dictation at certain levels, are inherently dangerous to the profound demands of personal responsibility. The highest responsibilities in life are personal. There is a point in human existence beyond which human dictation or organizational dictation ought not to extend.

But this seemingly individualistic idea that no man or organization has the unquestioned right to mediate between a man and his Creator is fraught with hidden dangers. Individuals and societies simply cannot get along without a guiding authority. When the authority of the church is removed, what other restraining and directing force can take its place? The great danger is anarchy. Has not this condition, for example, actually developed in American education? The extension of the Reformation revolt against the Roman Catholic Church has evolved into the modern pragmatic pseudo-Protestant revolt against practically everything.

Obviously the Reformers had no intention of instigating this kind of anarchistic chain of events. For Reformation faith the sovereign God assumed the place of rightful authority in place of a decadent church. God and truth and authority are accessible by each person through the Bible rather than through the church primarily.

There must be a freedom to discover God and truth and authority personally. The personal discovery of God and authority are the foundation stones for a truly free society. This does not mean that individuals ought not to be subject to the dictations of organizations, including the church, or churches, and the state, nor does this mean that the church is not essential to man's personal spiritual development. Men ought to respect and obey the higher powers. Christians ought to be supremely loyal to their church and its disciplines. Yet basically man circumvents external authorities in his most essential contact with God and His authority. This is the Reformation idea about the person, and it sets the stage for the Reformation concept of responsibility in education. The idea of responsibility is inextricably associated with the undefinable mystery of the existence of the person created in the image of God. And when God is eliminated from education, the only proper foundation for developing truly responsible persons is likewise eliminated. Pragmatic secularism in modern education quite significantly emphasizes educational principles which are similar to this Reformation point of view with one tragic exception: Relationships between man and man are substituted for the Reformation emphasis upon the prior relationships between man and God. Self-other relationships are substituted for the Reformation doctrine of the divine-human encounter. This secularization of Reformation faith leads to a dangerous kind of antirationalism which is abhorrent to both the Thomist and the classical humanist. In this respect the Thomist believes his synthesis of faith and reason provides a much safer balance for modern society. If men are taught to respect reason as well as to use it, the temporal world has a means to formulate authoritative procedures which prevent it from flying to pieces when irrationalism and relativism threaten its stability. Furthermore, man by nature is always in quest of certainty, and the emphasis upon reason as an integral part of human nature satisfies this quest. Societies can be much more easily stabilized when men recognize the validity of natural law as discovered by reason. The place to teach men to recognize this validity of reason is in school. And with the Catholic faith, Christian education is fundamentally in harmony with the life of reason because reason is God's creative form for the human person. Reason is good, and reason provides the reliable means to a well-ordered society.

Reformation faith agrees that reason is important in education, but nevertheless reason is also sinful and cannot be relied upon in the way the Thomists trust it. The Neo-Reformation theologians say that the tendency toward irrationalism ought not to be associated with Reformation Christian faith but rather with the decline of faith in God as the basis of personal existence. Irrationalism is a result of revolt: first, revolt by man against God and second, revolt of man within himself. Irrationalism is not the result of a rejection of the Aristotelian and Thomistic idea of rational substance pervading man's nature, but rather the result of a disrupted relationship between the whole person and God, and this disruption prevents the proper relationship between reason, will, and feeling within. By all means a rational emphasis in education is important today, but its promotion ought to come primarily through a readjustment of basic relationships and not primarily through the actualization of potential reason which the Thomists consider to be the basis of the human in man. The faith of the Reformers points to the restoration of proper relationships between the whole man and his Creator, and consequently the restoration of a proper balance between reason and will and feeling in the person, which in turn provides the means toward responsible relationships between persons and their neighbors.

Catholic and Reformation views of the communal significance of man's existence also lead to practical disagreements of considerable import. Again the primary division involves ideas about the nature of the church as a human community. Neo-Reformation faith places unusual emphasis upon the communal as well as the individual nature of man's fall. Men in a collective sense share in the guilt of the fall, and the communal refutation of God's order for the good community life is even harder for man to cope with than his own individual perversities. Communal and social movements are exceedingly powerful but also exceedingly dangerous in view of their power. Catholic faith might agree, but would except the church. The Roman Catholic Church, though made up of sinful men, is in some supernatural sense a sinless institution. But Reformation faith cannot be optimistic about the church's special category of sinlessness. When the church becomes powerful, the human tendency toward organizational perversion is particularly subtle and subversive. And this Reformation conviction suggests yet another reason for its traditional objections to final authority vested in the church as related to the cultural activities of the community, and to education in particular.

Because of conflicting views between Catholic and Reformation faith about the essential nature of man, there follows an inevitable disagreement about the nature of human sinfulness and about the function of the church in renewing the individual so that in principle he is capable of working out his salvation in history. Likewise, the Catholic concept of man as the image of God and as the likeness of God—so dignifying his reason on the one hand and making possible the restoration of the supernature by the church on the other hand, and therefore positing man as capable of perfectly knowing the truth and proceeding authoritatively in the light of this truth—is not acceptable to Reformation faith.

These disagreements about the nature of man make a cooperative Christian venture in community education almost an impossibility today. Are there any alternatives to this

seemingly inevitable deadlock within the center of Christendom—this deep cleavage which more than any other factor
seems to frustrate an effective program for the restoration
of the education of the community to its godly heritage?
Are there any practical means of supplying education once
again with a faith desperately needed in its task of developing responsible persons?

CHAPTER TWELVE

Education and Neo-Reformation Christian Faith

A MERICA'S whole cultural history, it has been noted, has a significant Protestant orientation, with early Calvinistic influences playing a leading role. With Protestantism so strongly a part of the American tradition, it is reasonable to suppose that a new Protestantism is significantly related to contemporary life with its crucial spiritual problems. As *Time* in a recent editorial says, the critical problem for America is to discover the means of bolstering moral progress so that it can catch up with material progress. Perhaps, writes *Time,* the most significant movement in this direction for "predominantly Protestant U. S. is the recent movement to restate and strengthen Protestant philosophy and theology."[1]

Reformation faith is also considered significant to contemporary American education because of its dynamic relationship to the early development of public education in America. The historical relationship between Protestantism and public education is nowhere more clearly demonstrated than in the educational history of the New England colonies. This faith, so distinguished for its early educational achievements, ought, in its present resurgence, to be reasonably considered for its powers of creative restoration.

Moreover, the twentieth century may distinguish itself in a most awesome way as another of those centuries of new birth, an age of unusual travail, possibly more tragic than ever before because of the new physical power at man's

[1] *Time* (March 9, 1953), 60.

disposal. Yet in a century of unusual turmoil Augustine made his great contribution, and likewise the Reformers, following in the theological footsteps of St. Paul. In times like these, men seem more prone to consider seriously the usually somewhat unpopular Christian acclamation of the sovereignty of God and the sinfulness of man.

At present this new Protestant orthodoxy is more vocal and more vital in Europe than in America, because Continental Christianity is in a position to be more directly aware of the disintegrative forces which threaten the world. For great sections of Europe these times are already violent, with the paralyzing specter of totalitarianism an immediate reality. Tragedy in Europe may explain the extreme theological position of Karl Barth in Germany, who, in his militant reaction against the intolerable evils of his culture, emphasizes anew the message of "man's impotence in the face of Supreme Righteousness."[2] Barth's neo-orthodoxy exemplifies an extreme Protestant reaction against the kind of radicalism which eventually regresses into "systems" degrading the worth of the individual and magnifying the supreme importance of the state. This new emphasis on the sovereignty of God is surely one of Christianity's most dynamic and radical defenses against the present world trend toward totalitarianism and collectivism. And it is not surprising that such a defense is at first most vigorously formulated in those areas where "systems" have revealed themselves in their most diabolical forms.

And so, because the core of American religious tradition is Protestant, because Reformation theology permeates the core of the Protestant contribution to public education in America, and finally because the temper of the times in this twentieth century is radical, the new Protestantism is assumed to be a significant emerging moral force in the world today, possessing a unique competency to counteract the

[2] John H. Randall, *The Making of the Modern Mind* (Boston, 1940), 569.

mounting challenges of collectivism and totalitarianism—challenges which more and more involve the deliberate educational processes of the nation.

Roman Catholicism appears at present the most powerful anticommunist religious force in that it is capable of opposing organizational force with similar organizational force. Its main defect, however, from the Reformation point of view, is that Catholicism itself is a great system, and the Neo-Reformation faith is fearful of any great system, good and powerful though it may be. The Reformed understanding of the radical nature of sin assumes that any powerful organization, whether the church or the state, is ever subject to great and terrible perversions. Accumulated power of any kind, even though in good faith it considers itself the representative of God, is nevertheless subject to the subtle perversions of lust for power for power's sake. Reformation Christian faith chooses not to answer the dark challenges of evil systems with counter systems primarily, but with personal faith. For Reformed Protestantism the real battlefield of the world remains the battlefield of the human soul. The primary battle with evil is a personal battle. Organizational power cannot be substituted for this personal encounter with sin and with the deepest realities of human life and destiny. The highest sovereignty for a man can never be that of an organization, a state, or a church, but only the sovereignty of God, this to be recognized as a personal act of faith. Of course, to make the personal relationship of every man to God primary does not, in this sinful world, annul the realistic need for organization and law in the name of justice. It does, however, accent the order of importance as between the individual and the state or the church.

Besides Karl Barth, the prophetic figure in Germany who rediscovers the "transcendent God of Calvin and His liberating Word," there are more moderate theological representatives of this Reformation movement, such as Emil Brunner, a theologian from Zurich, Switzerland (now in Japan), who writes and teaches in a more temperate mood without sacrificing the central theme of the Reformation tradition. He is more the theologian of proportion and moderation, dealing more generously with the motives and the fruits of human science and reason. Brunner is considered an important guide in this review of the relationships of the new Protestantism to public education. In America, Reinhold Niebuhr may be considered the neo-orthodox counterpart of Emil Brunner.

In this review of Reformation Christian faith and education it should be acknowledged immediately that history is not expected to repeat itself in the sense that Reformed Protestantism will soon become the creative force which permeates and restores to health the slumping form of twentieth century public education. In the first place the response today by society as a whole to Christian faith is mild compared to the times of the early Puritans in New England, when a theocracy was literally within the realm of possibility. Today the whole society is predominantly secular, and the school reflecting faithfully the *status quo* of its society can hardly be anything else. The impact of the new Protestantism, if it proves itself significant, can hope at best to begin reversing the dangerous trend toward secularism, by saying more clearly and forcefully that God is a Person and that He is sovereign over all, that He is "a Spirit, infinite, eternal and unchangeable in His being, wisdom, power, holiness, justice, goodness and truth."[3]

The mood of Reformation faith is not revolutionary in relationship to social or political organization. It is revolutionary only in respect to interpretation of the meaning of the person individually. The idea of "leavening" or "savoring" outlines the primary appointment of Christianity as the supporter and the regenerator of the existing order. This idea is explicitly not in accord with the more radical revolutionary impulses of some of the socialistic theorists intent

3 *The Shorter Catechism* (Philadelphia, 1941), 3.

upon pulling down strongholds in order to build some new kind of utopian world.

In education, for example, there are many advances associated with the nineteenth and twentieth century liberal impulse which ought to be recognized. Pragmatic influences have undoubtedly acted as a corrective in reference to both the Christian tradition and the classical tradition which failed in many cases to renew themselves in meeting modern challenges and thereby became formal and relatively unproductive. It is the task of Neo-Reformation Protestantism not to carry on a reactionary program against progressive methods when they have proven themselves—particularly in the elementary levels where the child is more correctly being understood as a dynamic individual rather than a passive receptacle—but to counteract that aspect of the liberal impulse which exemplifies a regressive movement from a supernaturalistic faith, particularly evident during the last hundred years. Pragmatism today, as a notable end product of this regression, is an example of a theological form divested of theological power. The contemporary American democratic faith, as a liberal expression, is in heavy debt to Protestantism, but it is also true that the prophets of the religion of humanity after 1865 tried to purge "the democratic pattern of the theological survivals it contained."[4] It seems impossible to deny the fact that "indeed 'nature' has silently displaced God as the ultimate basis to which all other things are referred."[5] There are features of modern education which are admirable and good. Yet there is needed the Christian attempt to re-present a challenging faith in the sovereign God who has been consciously or unconsciously, deliberately or carelessly, displaced or misplaced in the expansive, ebullient, philosophical educational transformations of the past century.

4 Gabriel, *The Course of American Democratic Thought,* 330.
5 Walter Moberly, *The Crisis in the University* (London, 1951), 138.

Certainly this problem of authority points up the critical conflict between the Pauline-Augustinian-Calvinistic Christian tradition and modern pragmatism. The Reformation view in this sense is radical: God is sovereign; God is the Authority. For the pragmatist, in contrast, there is no divine authority, and for some of the more radical pragmatic adherents, John Childs for example, supernatural faiths are actually a hindrance to democratic progress and ought to be dispelled as quickly as possible.

Yet the neo-orthodox Protestant insistence upon a faith in the sovereign God does not alienate Christian faith from experience. Surely there is no more consistent theme in the New Testament than the teaching that a tree is known by its fruits;[6] that "hearing" and "seeing" and "looking" are intimately related to the basic issues of life. Possibly the most profound and central truth of the Scriptures is the statement that "the *Word* was made flesh and dwelt among us."[7] Constantly there is the scriptural implication that faith without works is dead, being alone. The New Testament seems to be unique in its remarkable emphasis on the idea that the Word must become flesh, that faith should fulfill itself in practice, that the idea should fulfill itself in the act. It becomes quite explicit that a Christian critique of modern pragmatism does not create any fundamental schism concerning experience in itself, but rather applies to the pragmatic elimination of the spiritual origin and meaning of life and experience, namely of God the Creator and Preserver of all mankind.

The question of authority, being basic as it is, points up a second critical conflict between Reformation faith and modern pragmatism, namely, the question of what is truth. This problem is projected to the practical level in the question of the relationship of scientific truth to religious faith. Emil Brunner insists that within the Protestant theological framework there is a full recognition of the two concepts of truth

---

6 For example, Matthew 13:23 or 7:16-20.   7 John 1:14.

involved in the Christian-pragmatic disagreement about the nature of truth. Brunner says the early church made an unfortunate mistake in not distinguishing between what he calls "world-truth" and "God-Truth."[8] The medieval church unwisely censored men who were interested in discovering "world-truth," and this attitude by the church eventually engendered a powerful reaction so that today "world-truth" (scientific truth or pragmatic truth) has virtually eclipsed "God-Truth."

World-truth or pragmatic truth concerns itself primarily with the empirically understood universe. In the Christian view God created this universe and instituted the orders which maintain it. Furthermore, it is good for man to concern himself about the universe in which he lives. It is his to learn about, to investigate, to subdue. Science is a noble calling—a worthy and exciting calling. Yet scientific truth or world-truth can only be the rational, intellectual discovery of facts, laws, principles. This truth is at best only a partial description of reality. Not only should there be a concern about the nature of the created world, but also about the Creator who made it. This Creator-truth, however, is not a scientific discovery but a personal discovery. It is come by through a meeting of persons, not by the searching of a person through the realm of things. This knowledge of the personal God, this God-truth, is revealed truth and comes not through reason or scientific method, but by faith. For the pragmatist, world-truth is ultimate; for practical purposes there is no truth above and beyond world-truth. For Neo-Reformation Christianity, world-truth is good and legitimate, but the highest truth is come by personally through faith. Yet there need be no conflict between these two areas of truth discovery. The conflict arises when one area or the other is repressed.

8 Emil Brunner, *Christianity and Civilization* (2 vols., New York, 1948-1949), I, 36-38.

When the Reformation view of man and his destiny is compared with the outlook of the classical humanists, a different kind of basic contrast presents itself, involving dissimilarities which are of critical importance. When anyone tries to overemphasize the fundamental similarities between the Greek view and the Christian view, says Emil Brunner, he looks at the problem from such a distance that the whole picture is blurred.[9] The Greeks, in principle, start with humanity and proceed rationally to God. The Christian starts with God and from Him derives the meaning of man's humanity. With the Greeks man is the center (imbued, of course, with the divine principle) ; with the Christian, the Reformation view certainly, God is the center. On the one hand Reason is supreme, a principle which even supersedes the person; on the other hand the personal God stands supreme, the highest Truth, a Person, above reason. The classicists magnify the dictates of reason; the Christian acknowledges the will of God. In the one, reason comes first; in the other, revelation stands higher than reason. The one gives dominant support to the happiness of the elite; the other is primarily concerned with an expression of love to all, including the unlovely. The one, for example Socrates, chooses intelligence as the primary basis for the good; the other, for example Christ, decrees love as the highest meaning of the good. Biblical teachings emphasize that the primary aim of man is to do the will of God, but the Greeks stress the excellence of human nature.[10]

The Christian personal concept of God does not coincide with the Greek idea which tends to make God a divine principle immanent in the world and in man. With the Greeks the divine principle, Reason, makes the person. In Christian anthropology the person is not subservient to the

9 Emil Brunner, *Man in Revolt* (Philadelphia, 1947), 48-49.
10 A summary taken from Livingstone, *Greek Ideals and Modern Life,* 153-68.

divine principle, but prior to it. God is a Person; if there be principles, they proceed from Him.

This concept of God as the eternal Person delineates a distinctive relationship of God to the world and God to man, quite different from the Greek humanistic point of view. If God is a Person, He does not pervade the created universe primarily as a divine principle or impersonal law; He does not undergird man's humanity as the divine spark of reason dwelling immanent in the individual, but on the contrary, as a Person He exists uniquely separate and distinct from His creation and from man. God's significance to His creation and to man is His *relationship* to the created world and to man. God the Creator is a Person; He is the Subject. The created universe is impersonal; it is composed of things; it is objective. God through His infinite power and the orders of His creation momentarily sustains the created natural world. This is God's relationship as Subject to the objective natural world.

The Biblical emphasis upon the person stands in notable contrast to the classical emphasis. In the one case "person" is the highest principle; in the other case "reason" is the highest principle. For the Neo-Reformation theologian reason is an integral God-given part of the person, along with his will and feelings which are also God-given and essential. For the Greeks, by contrast, reason is clearly placed at the top of the hierarchy as the essential principle of humanity. The person is understood in terms of his reason, which is the divine principle underlying personality. In the classical view individuals are not persons in an infinite radical sense but are accidental expressions of the divine universal principle of reason. Hence the importance of "relationship" is limited, since with the Greeks the divine principle is a universal principle which does not set off one person against another in a radical manner but rather emphasizes the sharing of the common principle. In the Christian view, reason along with the will and the emotions constitutes the whole person who relates himself as a whole to other persons. For the classical humanist, reason is the primary principle of which all persons partake, and the relationship of person to person involves individual variations which are not radical but accidental. For the Christian every individual who bears a human face is not only the bearer of reason, but is a whole person created in the image of the divine Person. Every man is essentially a person whether he has rationally developed the divine spark or not. Every person stands in mysterious and sacred relationship to his Creator and to his fellow men regardless of the status of his reasoning abilities. The existence of the poor, the humble, and even the un-lovely is sacred because they are persons, in personal rela-tionship to God and to man. The rational principle in the Christian viewpoint is not the essential determining factor of man's humanity, whereas in the classical outlook this seems to be the case.

In spite of these radical differences between the faiths of the classical humanist and the neo-orthodox Christian, there is one extremely important aspect, at least, in which these two views coincide. They commonly testify to the humanity of man in terms of a human nature which partakes of a transcendent reality. Man is human because he possesses the qualitatively distinctive capacity to stand above the natural continuum. Christianity and Greek humanism present a solid front against all forms of naturalism which presuppose man's humanity to be contained within the natural sphere only.

A comparative review of Reformation Christian faith and educational reconstructionism highlights yet another series of similarities and some basic differences. Tawney observes that Calvinists and the more radical socialists are similar in that they all consider themselves chosen people, predestined to perform an all-important mission in the world. Tillich, in comparing orthodox Christianity and Marxism, says that they are similar in that both are deeply concerned with history and its end, both have a pessimistic sense of sin, both look toward goals of peace and justice, both have a deepened sense of catastrophe, and both agree that man exists in a fallen state, either because of original sin or because of a maladjusted society.[11] Both Reformation faith and reconstructionism acknowledge the basic importance of the irrational part of man's nature (or the "unrational" as Brameld calls it). The Christian labels the "irrational" as a good part of man which has become perverted; the reconstructionists classify the "unrational" as a nonmoral force that needs harnessing for moral purposes.

A polar distinction between the Neo-Reformation view and reconstructionism has to do with the nature of evil. The Christian understanding of evil is that it is personal. The reconstructionist insists that evil basically stems from the society. The one says that the person is in "revolt." The other says that the person is in revolt only because basically the society is in revolt. Reinhold Niebuhr, representing the Neo-Reformation view, has no confidence in social projects as a means of eliminating evil from the world. Niebuhr argues that every advance toward the good by man or by society is attended with an exposure to more subtle forms of perversion to which the good succumbs. Every increase in human knowledge brings greater evil as well as greater good. And group action is even more susceptible to evil perversion than individual action. Group morality is even more easily perverted than individual morality. Thus the collective and totalitarian ideals, modern socialistic schemes projected as the basis for the elimination of social evils, are hopeless and dangerous dreams. According to the Reformation's realistic view of man's sinful nature, there can be no utopia in this world. The optimistic progressive dreams of

11 Paul Tillich, *The Protestant Era* (Chicago, 1948), 254.

the perfectibility of man by social maneuver do not stand the test of reality. The contemporary radical hope that great power centered in some benevolent collective force shall be morally and physicaly strong enough to overcome the evils in the world must eventually frustrate itself at the sight of the great evils and injustices which flow from the collective force itself.

Yet the Christian is not pessimistic in the face of discouraging world events with all of the attendant evils, because the Christian way is the personal way, the way of faith in God, so that by the power of God man transcends the evil which he cannot overcome in his own strength. Here the basic positions of the Christian educator and the educational reconstructionist are polar, the one saying that God and no other is the answer to evil in the world, and the contrary position saying that man and no other can furnish a solution to this problem.

These positions become polar not only in theory but in practice when the collectivist systems come to the conclusion that any type of personal faith contrary to that of the "system" is a serious deterrent to the system in reaching its self-appointed objectives for society. This observation seems to apply to any totalitarian regime, *whether church or state*. Man-made systems in the name of god probably provided first-rate historical models for the twentieth century man-made systems in the name of man. In any case a personal loyalty to a Sovereign higher than the system becomes a stumbling block to the designs of the system, and eventually the person must succumb to the system or suffer unfortunate consequences. And yet, insists the Christian personalist, the freedom of the person to choose his sovereign loyalty is the foundation of a good society. Many a modern radical social reformer, Toynbee observes, is purging out as best he can the very spiritual faculty by which man can know the true nature of man and God and sin.

The grave danger to the personal concept of the nature of man latent in the collectivist trend, whether democratic or autocratic, can best be discovered by looking at the roots of the radical, naturalistic form of democracy which has emerged as a full-fledged religious faith in support of collectivistic programs. Rousseau seems to be an early champion of this non-Christian form of equalitarian democracy. Rousseau's concept of democracy was non-Christian first of all because he replaced the sovereignty of God with the sovereignty of the general will. The general will, expressed in practical form as majority will, he identified with the infallible right, with the assertion that *nothing* must stand between the individual and his duty to the state. For this reason Rousseau considered Christianity a radical vice—a constant source of dissension impeding the democratic process.[12]

In the light of this background, the Neo-Reformation theologian is impelled to examine critically all modern expressions of the democratic faith, especially those which clearly show their discontinuity with supernatural faiths. Evidently a proposed democratic way of life substantiated by a naturalistic faith is radically different from a democratic way of life based upon a Christian faith in the sovereignty of God. At least two widely divergent streams of democratic thought and faith become distinguishable, the one rationally and scientifically founded upon the sovereignty of man, and the other personally founded upon the sovereignty of God. From the point of view of Reformation faith the difference between these two outlooks is radical. One basic consideration, however, is common to all views and is highlighted in the simple question: What makes man human? Each philosophical position seriously proposes an answer to this question; hence the many kinds of humanists: classical, rational, scientific, and Christian. Karl Barth, in behalf of

[12] Sabine, "The Two Democratic Traditions," in *The Philosophical Review*, LXI (1952), 464.

the Christian humanists, defines the humanism of man in terms of the "humanism of God." In the Christian sense, the supreme basis of humanism is God incarnate. The practical expression of humanism is love for fellow man, sacrificial love, genuine love for the unlovely as well as the lovely. As Augustine puts it, man's humanity depends not on his intelligence but on what he loves, and what a man loves makes an infinite amount of difference to the status of his humanity. "For every civilization, or every period in history it is true to say: 'Show me what kind of god you have, and I will tell you what kind of humanity you possess.' "[13] It seems only logical, for example, that the heathen worshipers of Molech, the god of fire, should eventually sacrifice their children by burning them alive, or that pagan cults in their nature worship of fertility should eventually sexually desecrate human beings in their temples.

If it be true that man's humanity is based upon what he loves or worships, and that genuine humanism cannot be dissociated from the worship of the sovereign God, it follows that the continuing eradication of man's personal worship of God decrees a continuing depersonalization of man, a continuing deterioration of the kind of humanism to which all philosophies seem to subscribe. The modern naturalisms which describe man only as a complex animal who derives his human qualities from the natural environment are in danger of promoting the grossest kind of inhumanity. Christian humanism therefore insists that "it is imperative to understand once more that the rediscovery of man will also be the rediscovery of God. That is the essential theme of Christianity."[14]

Neo-Reformation humanism, based upon man's personal faith in God, is eloquently presented in Dr. Baillie's *Invitation to Pilgrimage,* where he quotes the French writer E. Doumergue on this essential theological tenet of Reformed

---

[13] Brunner, *Man in Revolt,* 34.
[14] Nicolas Berdyaev, *Solitude and Society* (London, 1938), 152.

Protestantism: "It is . . . the theologies of the enslaved will which have saved liberty; it is the theologies of salvation by another than man which saved human morality; it is the theologies of renunciation of the world which have saved man's mastery over the world; it is the theologies of man's renunciation of himself which have saved human personality; it is the theologies that preached love toward God alone which have saved love towards all men; it is the theologies of eternal predestination which have saved progress; . . . it is the theologies that said, 'God is all, man is nothing' which have made man a force, an energy, a power incomparable and divine."[15]

With these distinctive Christian elaborations of the nature of God and the nature of man, Reformation faith is urgently concerned with the problem of the relationship of God to education in America today. For surely education is a moral venture, fundamentally concerned with this all-encompassing quest for the basis of man's humanity. If the Christian concept of God is basically related to man's humanity, it must be radically considered in its relation to man's education.

In the earlier days American education was not so directly confronted with the problem of God in education, because the whole society was permeated to a certain extent with Christian faith in God. It was not considered hypocritical at that time, apparently, that even American currency ought to be a witness to this faith: "In God We Trust." Not only the Christian church, but the home and the school were generally strong in this common faith. Today America no longer possesses to the same degree this common godly faith. The former theological support to both home and school for the educational task of developing responsible persons is now greatly weakened, and the moral vacuum left in its wake has indeed precipitated a contemporary educational

[15] John Baillie, *Invitation to Pilgrimage* (New York, 1942), 104.

crisis. As a result there are today many movements in education to develop moral and spiritual values programs; a new flood of books and articles is being written on the contemporary problem of education and morals; discussions about the problem are prominent in many educational meetings and conventions. The schools must have working answers to these problems, or else the community tends to fall apart. And it seems, regardless of the philosophical starting point for the solutions of those problems, there is always posed the primary question of "faith." Faith in what—democracy, or some kind of "ism," or God?

Actually the problem of education and faith is itself indeed a dilemma. Both liberal nonsectarians and orthodox Protestants have been generally firm in their insistence of the separation of church and state. Particular faiths must not be allowed to utilize public education as sounding boards for their own special interests. This is, in fact, against the law. Yet how can education today operate without a basic faith upon which it itself rests and by which it is guided? How can education as a moral venture say what ought to be, without a faith to help it? Because of this pressing need many progressive educators, and the radical educators more boldly, have formulated a democratic, secular faith which they believe is quite in accord with the spirit of the times and which supports the proposition that all men have a right to certain basic freedoms, including the freedom from religious imposition in the educational process.

But here the real dilemma comes more clearly into focus. The democratic faith which men propose as the underlying faith for twentieth century American education is itself, by virtue of its naturalistic origins, an imposition and a violation of conscience for that segment of the citizenry which yet adheres to a faith in God and seeks the same for its children. The principle of separation of church and state, designed to protect the religious sensibilities of its citizens, including non-Christians, from the danger of imposition and violation of conscience, is here again faced, but in reverse order. The new danger is that a *non-Christian* democratic faith shall violate the conscience of many who yet adhere to a Christian faith in the sovereign God.

The dilemma is that education must have a faith in order to fulfill its moral task in society, but this faith ought not to be officially motivated by any particular sectarian or secular group which violates the religious conscience of any minority. Yet this assumption seems to imply that education can have no faith at all in our American society of heterogeneous faiths. But an education without faith is meaningless if its primary assignment in the twentieth century is considered a moral assignment: the development of good men, good citizens, good workmen.

And so, from the Neo-Reformation point of view, the problem of God in education is critical, for if education cannot proceed upon faith in God, it must be guided by some other faith; education must have its faith. And the Neo-Reformation concept of the nature of man cannot allow it to express any confidence in a naturalistic, nontheological faith as the basis for an education which is to succeed in the face of contemporary problems where the hope of a free society is at stake. In other words, Neo-Reformation faith insists that the problem of developing responsible persons in education requires a theological solution.

Chapter Thirteen

A Theological Solution to the Problem of Developing Responsibility

THE IMPLICATIONS of personal responsibility are not so profound in a closed society, either primitive, with its set frame for determining men's activities, or totalitarian in the modern sense, where the state makes the critical choices and the individual simply defers to the state. But in our open society with its framework of individual freedom as outlined by the Greeks and vitalized by the Christian faith in Western culture, personal responsibility becomes at once a great glory and a heavy cross.[1] Western civilization has drunk deeply of the wine of individual freedoms, and the thought of losing these freedoms seems unbearable.

In the Western Hebrew-Christian tradition a free society is hardly conceivable apart from free persons who constitute it. And persons cannot long remain free unless they use their freedoms responsibly. Individual responsibility is surely to be discovered a fundamental factor at the base of an open society. On the other hand, the personal freedoms which the Western world holds priceless, along with its ideal of the infinite worth of the individual, seem uniquely sensitive to the deteriorating effects of individual irresponsibility. Personal irresponsibility, from a Reformation Christian point of view at least, is to be discovered at the base of the growing threats of totalitarianisms and collectivisms. If an open society is to be defended against the increasing non-Christian collectivistic entrenchments, there must be a revitalization

[1] Karl R. Popper, *The Open Society and Its Enemies* (2 vols., London, 1945), I, 176.

of the essential cohesive forces which hold together an open, free society.[2]

The dilemma for an open society is that these cohesive forces cannot be external forces primarily, for if they are, they violate the principles of personal freedom with which the free world is now so seriously concerned. Because an open society is not organized along the lines of close and detailed regulation of the activities of its citizens, the element of personal irresponsibility is all the more devastating. A free society is relatively unprotected against the temptations of many kinds of personal irresponsibilities. When a person is free to the extent that he can be responsible in a higher sense of the word, he invariably possesses a greater freedom to be irresponsible. In a free society there exists a minimum of rigid custom; there are few policies of the mailed fist to check irresponsibilities which violate specific laws. An open society, therefore, finds itself in really serious straits when more and more members utilize their freedoms irresponsibly.

The force which holds a free society intact must be, it seems, some kind of inner conviction. This inner virtue, according to the Neo-Reformation view, is personal responsibility. Neo-Reformation theology insists that the current trend toward personal irresponsibility in free communities can, in the long run, best be counteracted by the rediscovery of the radical meaning and origin of this human capacity called responsibility; that the true meaning of responsibility is to be discovered and substantiated theologically; that historical formulations of personal freedom and personal responsibility are concomitants of vital Christian faith; that there is a significant relationship between the decline of personal responsibility of free persons in open societies and the decline of theological faith in all realms of life; and finally,

2 An open society is described by Popper as a society in which individuals are confronted with personal decisions.

that the relationship between Christian theology and the
concepts of freedom and responsibility are so basic that no
amount of substituted activity, good though it may be in
itself, such as social planning or the erudite explorations of
the meaning of values or the application of the scientific
method to morals, can in the long run hold the line in supporting an open society. Though planning and collective
measures in the twentieth century world seem necessary,
their primary purpose ought to be that of stopgap measures,
holding actions, so that free peoples may yet use the freedoms they possess to discover the deeper truths needful in
the development of responsible persons. And it is the view
of Neo-Reformation faith that the twentieth century renewal of the Biblical concept of the sovereignty of God with
its concomitant belief about the sinful nature of man is the
starting point in the support and vitalization of personal
responsibility needed for the continuance of a free society.

The meaning of responsibility and irresponsibility is so
fundamental in a Christian sense that they cannot be dissociated from the deepest origins of human personality. And
these origins, theologically speaking, are supratemporal, supernatural, founded in the Being of the eternal Person.
Responsibility, in its deepest meaning, is grounded in a
positive relationship between the person and his Creator.
Irresponsibility has its roots in negative relationship between
person and Creator, which is simply another way of speaking
about the dogma of the fall of man, or original sin. The
highest degree of responsibility, in this setting, is understood
as charity in action: love. Yet this does not define responsibility, for the supreme meaning of love seems to transcend
all definition, as does the full meaning of freedom and
personality. In a practical sense, however, this power of
love does reveal itself as a kind of inner dynamic which constructively relates a person to his neighbor. This basic rela-
tional power is the spiritual texture of a free community,

and it is the Christian conclusion that this supremely needful element of human existence can only be understood theologically.

Yet, according to the Neo-Reformation concept of man's nature it must be acknowledged that some degree of responsibility exists in human beings regardless of their primitiveness, their culture, their religion. Every man is created in the image of God. The creative order of man is a responsible order. Whatever the culture, man distinguishes himself in terms of his nature as a responsible being. In primitive societies where the potential for personal freedom is low, man understands his own nature only vaguely, and yet the concept of responsibility is there, else there would not be a human society. In the degree to which responsibility is understood as God's creative order for man's existence, the potentiality for an open society has been established. The fullest understanding of freedom and responsibility comes in the Christian theological concept of man created for free fellowship with God and with other persons, his neighbors. Yet, regardless of whether the society is Christian or not, regardless of the culture or the religion, men do evolve some type and degree of responsible relationships because they are created in the image of God. Responsibility in any form is theologically rooted, whether men are cognizant of it or not, because men's natures are grounded in God their Creator.

The real basis of a free community, then, according to Reformation faith, is that vital inner bent within the hearts of men which expresses itself practically through love in action. Yet this concept of love is never ideally fulfilled by man. Faith in God and its concomitant expression in love toward one's neighbor is always the act of sinful man in a sinful society. But even imperfect faith expressed in imperfect love by imperfect man effects a powerful influence upon the community of men, just as good salt has great powers of seasoning. Hence, in the Neo-Reformation view, one may strive toward the ideal of a free society without having to subscribe to some form of utopian ideology.

The basis of individual responsibility may be designated in the Christian sense as God's creative order of personal existence: man created in the image of God and created with the unique individual capacity to be personally responsible in his relationship to his Creator. A corollary to this creative personal design for man is the creative order of family existence: male and female in their creative human relationships. The "person" is not a changeable product of a natural environment but the eternal creation of the eternal God, and likewise the family is not a human institution which may be radically modified to suit the demands of the times. God's orders for human existence—orders which involve basic relationships to Him, and creative family relationships—are not to be modified to a changing environment, because they are divine orders. Ignorance or violation of these orders involves serious injury to persons and to the hope of their responsible development.

The proper consideration of these orders for human existence gives man the clue to the proper basis for the orderly community, of which education is an integral part. Such a consideration is extremely important today when society suffers from an unfortunate disruptive emphasis upon the importance of the individual on the one hand over against the importance of the group on the other. In the one case society is reduced more and more to an aggregate of "atomistic" individuals, and in the other case society becomes merely an organism with individuals as comparatively insignificant cells.[3] The Neo-Reformation emphasis of the divine "personal" order and the divine "family" order integrates this antithetical emphasis of the one and the many. The theological idea of the personal order of existence properly

---

[3] Arnold J. Toynbee, *A Study of History,* abridged by D. C. Somervell (New York, 1947), 576.

acknowledges the infinite worth and dignity of the individual. At the same time the theological idea of the family order comprehends the root meaning of community. The life of the family, in practice, integrates the "one" and the "many" so that both are infinitely important and complementary to one another. These two orders, believed to be divinely instituted and supported, constitute the basis for the Neo-Reformation idea of an education which can truly concern itself with the problem of developing the kind of personal responsibility needed to support and maintain a free society.

Johann Pestalozzi, a teacher in Switzerland during the latter part of the eighteenth century, was one of the most illustrious educational exponents of this idea that the family order most effectively takes into account the problems involved in educating for responsibility. At best, said Pestalozzi, the larger school constitutes a husk around the kernel which the child has received at home. At the beginning of the child's educational venture there is no teacher who can take the place of the mother. The highest aim of education, he insisted, is the emphasis upon love and faith which begins in the relationship of mother to child and ends in relationship of the person to his Creator and Redeemer.[4] The concept of love as the basic foundation for a proper education was emphasized over and over again in Pestalozzian educational philosophy. However, it was not a concept of an abstract love, but love in activity, an inclusive kind of personal expression which involves head, hand, and heart.

The strength of the larger community is to be discovered, according to Pestalozzi, in the strength of the home; the vitality of the education in the larger community is directly related to the vitality of the education in the home. And since the home is irreplaceable, one of the prime responsibilities of the larger community educational ventures should

4 Lewis Flint Anderson, *Pestalozzi* (New York, 1931), 28-34, 216-17.

be the positive and aggressive support of home and family. "In order to promote the education of the people it is above all necessary to revive in parents the conviction that they possess the ability to promote the education of their children."[5] The regeneration of the community comes not by "endowments, legislation, or by new methods, important as these are, but, as Pestalozzi thought, by love and devotion of noble women overflowing from the domestic circle into the community."[6]

These Pestalozzian views on education constitute a significant starting point for the Neo-Reformation ideas about modern education. The family must be the foundation of an education which truly takes the "person" seriously. The family order makes possible the deepest understanding of responsible "I-thou" relationships. And the Christian family provides the real foundation for community education. The best kind of community education is the direct extension of family education. This kind of an educational foundation makes possible a free community, because persons, learning the profound meaning of responsibility at the most completely personal family level and the next most personal community level, possess the kind of vitality necessary for fulfilling their obligations responsibly to all levels of community existence.

Of course, it is much easier to contemplate than to demonstrate the ideal education in an ideal community. As usual, there is today much that is unsatisfactory about the educational setting provided by the larger society. Today's community, generally speaking, no longer appears to be founded upon any common faith, let alone a common Christian faith. Possibly this whole idea of an education based upon a Christian personal concept of the nature of man is quite visionary in the face of the cold realities of the collective trend accen-

5 Anderson, 135.
6 Eva Channing (trans.), *Leonard and Gertrude,* by Johann Pestalozzi (Boston, 1885), vii.

tuated by a mechanized and industrialized environment. Furthermore, seeing how prone education is to reflect the *status quo* of its society, is it not unrealistic to think of an education theologically undergirded within a larger community which has for the most part lost its theological orientation?

In response to the implication that this Reformation emphasis on educational fundamentals tends to be utopian, it should be pointed out that the Reformation tradition is extremely realistic about the nature of man. The moment the Christian faith becomes sentimental and dreams about evolving the good life and the good society in some ideal form, it deviates sharply from its basic Christian dogma about the radical nature of evil in man. Yet an expression of its pessimism is also an expression of its optimism. Reformation faith is convinced that man in history has always clearly demonstrated his sinful ways, and that he continues to do so today, and that within the natural course of history he will continue to do so. This conclusion is the pessimistic aspect of the Reformation tradition. Yet, paradoxically, where this tradition has been strongest, open societies have come into existence. Free societies have not, in history, evolved from ideal conditions; actually they have developed within the confines of unideal cultures. This conviction is Reformation optimism.

Comparatively free societies do exist. The American way of life is a notable example. Yet surely the American way of life was not born and fostered in an ideal setting. Any society in any age seems to be characterized by a goodly share of aberrant and questionable features. American culture at its best is beset with many sins and shortcomings, social injustices, moral blind spots.

The question of the practicality of a contribution of Neo-Reformation faith, therefore, ought not to be decided upon the basis of the ideality or unideality of the contemporary moral and spiritual climate. Not the determination of the existing environment but the vitality of a faith would seem to be the basic feature which determines a successful and effective contribution to the present needs of education. A vital faith ought to gain significance in its relation to difficult problems simply because it need not be vitiated by subversive environmental influences.

What, then, are some of the specific contributions which a Christian faith may offer to a society and an education which is not necessarily Christian in its perspective? What does a Christian faith with its strong emphasis upon the personal nature of man and the divinely instituted family order as the basis of a good education have to say to a secular and public order of education in a free society which is now in jeopardy?

In response to these questions it should be made clear that the examination of the relationship of Christian faith to public education is not primarily to be concerned at this point with specifics of the educational process: administrative and instructive procedures, methods, programs, and the like. The primary concern here is the philosophical setting in which education proceeds with its practical duties.

In the first place, Neo-Reformation Christianity has a positive contribution to make to its society in its re-emphasis upon the worth of tradition. An essential need for our time is the restoration of a greater respect for law and order. This emphasis is particularly significant to the modern educational program. One of the volatile characteristics of the contemporary age is the widespread revolt against all kinds of authority, and especially against tradition as an authority. In this revolt there seems little doubt that pragmatic doctrines take the lead, founded as they are in the teachings of John Dewey whose theme of revolt against tradition seems to qualify him as the protestant of protestants.

Public education cannot effectively serve the community so long as it remains in a constant state of revolt, where tradition and the individual dynamic stand in "either-or" relationship. Christian faith offers a mediating influence in this conflict because Christianity in essence is tradition, and Christianity in essence is also a recognition of the dynamic appropriative nature of the individual. The Reformation of course is unique for its recognition of the God-given rights of the individual over against a false tradition. But certainly the Reformation was not antitraditional. Modern pragmatic doctrines are the consequence of a one-sided emphasis upon the dynamic of the individual. Reformation faith offers a doctrine which takes into account both the dynamic of the individual and the valid place of tradition in the educational process.

Directly connected with a revival of respect for tradition is the revival of a respect for the law. According to the Reformers, men ought to obey the law because it is an order for society which God approves. So long as the government allows a workable degree of freedom for men, the Christian best serves his country, his government, and its agencies, including the schools, by seeking to conserve them and to respect the persons who represent them. Discipline in the schools is an increasingly frightful problem which is sapping the morale of many teachers and administrators. According to the Reformation point of view, godly fear is not only the beginning of wisdom but the foundation for the effective maintenance of discipline. And without discipline there can hardly exist an education worthy of the name.

In this respect Reformation faith tends to align itself with the classical emphasis on discipline and reason in the learning process. The recognition of the importance of law almost necessarily involves a parallel acknowledgment of discipline and reason in the educative program. The Reformation, of course, interprets the New Testament message to mean that neither reason nor the law can save mankind. But this conclusion does not detract from the practical importance of the work of law and reason in a sinful world, the life of which obviously is not based upon the standards of love alone; a world wherein love ought to prevail but does not, and where the practical expedient of law based upon reason must be depended upon. A friendly attitude toward a stronger emphasis on law and reason in education is quite apparent in denominations which have not moved far from orthodox Reformation theology, as, for example, the Christian Reformed Church with its strong Calvinistic predilection or the Presbyterian Church in the United States, which is now saying that there ought to be a powerful renewal of the life of reason in its higher educational institutions. One of the preliminary conclusions of the North Carolina Presbyterian Synod Survey is that piety is not enough—which is but the reiteration of a long standing Scottish Presbyterian ecclesiastical sentiment.[7]

In the second place, Reformation Christian faith in its preoccupation with the family order as the basis of education, and the community family-of-families school as the logical extension of the family education, raises a critical voice against the modern trend toward standardization and consolidation in public education. Modern education seems bent on separating the child from his immediate environment in order to build up bigger and better schoolhouses for bigger and better systems all for less over-all costs and more efficiency. But Reformation Christian faith suggests that when the state more and more assumes a central place in education and when persons and communities more and more defer to it, there is a serious danger that what is intended to be personal in education becomes routinely impersonal. The best kind of education, according to Reformation faith, is founded upon a "spiritual federalism" as opposed to the radically socialistic utopian and often economically determined "spiritual centralism." There is always

7 A tentative conclusion presented by Roger McCutcheon, director of the Synod Survey of educational institutions in North Carolina, at the annual Synod meeting, July 14, 1954.

the real danger that great organizations, instead of being protectors of individual freedoms, become usurpers of them.

In at least one other respect the Reformation Christian idea of the family order as the basis for good education yields a significant commentary on modern educational trends. This comment applies to the Rousseauistic rationally formulated theory of egalitarianism which has now reached virile proportions in some modern circles of educational philosophy. Rousseau, and later Marx, and now many adherents of a radical democracy have made a fetish of the idea of equality. The principle of equality, they imply, is to be matched with the idea of justice; hence there should be a kind of revolutionary communistic equalizing trend in many areas of life, not only in economics, but in the realm of authority and government, in social relations, and even in methods of evaluation in education. The central hypothesis of the equalitarians seems to be that the principle of equality is so overwhelmingly the distinguishing feature of human existence, and inequalities are so comparatively unessential, that when men, being basically equal, are the unequal recipients of the various goods of life, injustice prevails.

The Christian answer to these egalitarian, radically democratic conclusions is the Christian concept of the family. The family, as a base unit of community, illustrates not only the essential meaning of *equality*, but also the fundamental significance of *inequality*. The unique value of inequality is that it enhances the significance of real community. A significant aspect of community, in a Christian sense, is the fact that people are different from one another and therefore really need one another. By contrast it would seem that the rationalistic emphasis upon equality engenders not community but independence. The whole basis of family life is endangered because marriage is not considered a profound union based upon mutual dependence, but a kind of contract between two equal parties.[8] The Christian idea suggests

8 The analysis of Emil Brunner in *Christianity and Civilization*, Book I.

that marriage is a vital communion because each party is different from the other in function and therefore each is dependent upon the other for his proper fulfillment. This concept of essential differences of function is not given proper consideration in modern equalitarian philosophies. In a Christian sense the family order illustrates both the infinite value of the individual and the differences of function of each individual, so that he is radically needed by other persons—and needs other persons—for a full personal life. And because persons, equal in the sight of God, are different in their functions and capacities, they ought so to be recognized, whether in the family, or in the school, or in the larger society, for these differences constitute an essential human need for community existence.

At this point possibly it is time to recall the particular problem in education which each of the previous educational theories, discussed in this book, were faced up to: the question of developing responsibility in education in connection with the relationships of racial groups in the community. The pragmatists argued that experience was the key to this problem. The classical humanists placed the emphasis upon reason, the one area where all races and all religions can find a common ground. The reconstructionists placed their confidence in group dynamics, beginning with the school as the hub and eventually extending outward into the whole community, so that through group discussion and group action all races and religious groups of the community learn properly to appreciate one another.

The Christian position in the light of the Christian definition of the profound basis of human responsibility suggests that what is most needful in establishing responsible relationships between groups and persons in any community is the positive personal relationship between neighbors which issues from a positive personal relationship between every man and his Creator. The man who is responsive to the eternal Person who created him is genuinely humble in his dealings with his neighbor. Right relationship to God is the basis for an "unjudging" and responsive relationship to other persons. Outstanding Negro leaders like Ralph Bunche have emphasized the "personal" aspect of the race problem, saying that the only truly satisfactory basis for an eventual solution of the problem lies in the multiplication of positive personal relationships between persons of each race. And this is in effect a conservative position in regard to the problem. Organized crusades and organized conflict fomented by radical forces lead to harmful circumstances for all concerned. An emphasis on the common ground of reason seems plausible, but men at large show little talent for rational procedure in the face of emotional aspects of race relationships. The pragmatic emphasis on common experience does not distinguish clearly enough between qualities of experience. Closer associations and common experiences can result in untoward as well as favorable relations. The common intermingling of American soldiers with many peoples in far parts of the world has not by any means demonstrated only positive gains in interracial understandings.

The Reformation explanation of the tendency of groups to maintain themselves at odds with one another suggests the deep basis of revolt between individuals and their Creator. The clearest evidence of this basic revolt is idolization of self. And the practical demonstration of this kind of perverse idolization is pride, a human capacity which more than any other leads one person to consider himself superior to others. When this attitude is intensified in the more irrational aspects of group relationships, nothing less can be expected than that underprivileged peoples get the unmistakable impression that they are considered means rather than ends. Because every person is in fact created a son of God and because he realizes himself as an end, every person regardless of his station is extremely sensitive to any attitude which values him as less than an end. In this respect Reformation faith is radical in its diagnosis of the problem: Only the proper relationships of persons to God can restore the proper relationships of groups one to the other.

But in another aspect Reformation faith is conservative in its attitude toward the problems of race relationships; it stands clearly opposed to radical socialistic programs intended to correct the problem on a mass scale. Social programs which are not founded upon the radical revolution within individual persons is doomed to failure, creating more havoc and grief than good. The little book of the New Testament called Philemon is the standard text for the Reformation concept of the basis of responsible relationships between the privileged and the underprivileged. The transformation of the personal relationship between the slave and his master is utterly radical. But the transformation of the social structure is considered by Paul a secondary matter which will right itself through the permeative quiet revolution which evolves from the transformation of personal relationships. From the Christian point of view it is not common experience primarily, nor reason essentially, nor group dynamics, but personal decision which provides the foundation for responsible relationships between persons and groups in the community. And personal decisions which support right relationships between a man and his neighbor are founded upon right relationships between a man and his Creator. These personal decisions are basically free decisions, and only the accumulation of these free decisions by persons can support a free society where men live responsibly one with the other.

There remains at least one momentous and difficult question which derives from the very heart of any discussion on the educational problem of developing responsible persons: the problem of church and state relationship, or stated in more challenging terms, the problem of religion in education. It seems inevitable, as has been mentioned before, that education cannot cope with twentieth century problems unless it is motivated by some kind of vital faith. Responsibility understood in its deepest sense seems to imply that it cannot be separated from faith. If a vital faith is important to education in general and to the development of responsible persons in particular, what kind of faith ought this to be? And if that faith ought to be Christian, how can it be made an integral part of a program of public education? At this point we are directly faced with the American principle of state and church separation.

Protestantism in America from the beginning was extremely sensitive to the religious injustices which it had experienced in the Old World. The forefathers of the new America were adamant in their insistence on church and state separation in order to avoid the crimes of religious imposition from which Americans had escaped often at great cost. It is therefore understandable that conservative Protestantism today continues to support this historical position for fear that once again some powerful religious organization will gain control of the state and eventually usurp a favorable position for imposing its faith through governmental power.

But the affirmation of the principle of church and state separation by Reformed Protestantism involves a practical dilemma in relation to the pressing educational problems of the day. One can hardly separate Christian faith from the denomination which propagates it. And the Reformed denominations cut themselves off from an influential impact upon public education by their specific affirmation of the validity of the principle of church and state separation. If education must have a faith to carry on its work effectively, and Christian denominations cannot officially supply education with such a faith, its only legitimate procedure seems to involve the development of a secular faith, a nonreligious faith against which there is no law in education. The churches cannot promote a program within education, and the schools in their desperate plight can hardly wait for the indirect influences of spiritual permeation from without. In considering this dilemma it ought to be observed that the historical nineteenth century development of the principle of church and state separation in the schools did not take into account an unforeseen twentieth century danger of the inroads of a secular faith of nontheological origin which is literally inimical to Christian faith. This twentieth century development in public education suggests for Christian faith at least two momentous alternatives: either a conclusion that the principle of church and state separation in education as traditionally outlined is becoming obsolete, or the conclusion that Christian faith can no longer positively support the traditional American institution of public education. If public education needs a faith, either Christian faith must discover effective methods of supporting public education or it must withdraw for fear that a democratic nontheological faith shall irreparably weaken Christianity through its secular influences upon the young.

The Roman Catholic Church in America is one segment of Christendom which has made its decision to withdraw from public education and to support a system of parochial schools for the purpose of nurturing and protecting the Christian faith of its young. Some of the conservative Protestant groups, notably the Christian Reformed Church, a traditionally strong Calvinistic denomination, have come to the same conclusion and have started their own parochial systems. But Neo-Reformation Christian faith on the whole seems yet to be deeply concerned with the support and conservation of the public school. What can this faith say to the dilemma which it faces in its support of the traditional separation of the public school from Christian denominations? If the problem of education for responsibility can only be solved by returning to God in education, as Reformation Christian faith clearly attests, how can an emphasis upon this theological reorientation become practical in the light of the present dilemma?

CHAPTER FOURTEEN

Education, the Community, and Christian Faith

CHRISTIAN faith, both Reformation and Catholic, agrees that education cannot be neutral about faith, that education by virtue of its moral and spiritual tasks must have its sustaining faith. And from the Christian point of view an education for the development of free and responsible persons cannot proceed upon nontheological premises. The modern Western world, therefore, simply cannot afford to neglect its Christian tradition and heritage. Neither the state nor education can fulfill its responsibility to our kind of a society without Christian foundations and Christian direction. Until the men of contrary opinion can demonstrate more satisfactory alternatives, both the state and education ought to acknowledge the positive relationship of Christian faith to the political and cultural vigor of a free community.

This viewpoint is obviously not acceptable to any kind of secularism which looks for the state to increase its activity and influence in modern education. On the other hand the state today is taking account of Christian faith in a manner that would have been considered hardly possible a few decades ago. Governmental representatives are giving unusual consideration to the work of Christian groups, and often official utterances are unapologetically theological. America is truly concerned these days in many quarters about its Christian heritage. If the state decides that a vital Christian faith ought to be genuinely acknowledged, the state should also grasp the significance of the Christian wisdom which repeatedly says the strength of a vigorous free society derives from a Christian faith and culture which develops upward through the family and the local community, and not through some kind of centralized program.

This Christian insistence upon the significance of the family life and the wholesome community life is a generalization to which both Reformation faith and Catholicism freely subscribe. The question of the restoration of the vigor of the local community is not these days any light matter. The present impact of communism is eloquent testimony to a crisis in the community. The current vigor of Marxist views about the meaning of the community are in one sense a disturbing indication of inherent weaknesses in our Western kind of individualism, which at best is only partly Christian. Powerful influences in our society conspire to separate man from man and to shatter the basis of the lively community. Nowhere is this tragic reaction more evident than in our rural communities and in smaller communities of all kinds, where the glamour of great cities destroys the local morale because both young and old prefer bigness and excitement to the small town. Yet with all the feverish pursuit of excitement and the desperate attempt to skirt the bogs of local boredom, the searcher gasps for spiritual refreshment because he does not know that genuine living is somehow tied up with communion with others sharing a common faith, common interests, sufferings, and achievements.

Christian faith has an answer to the problem of "community," although it certainly has done little in this twentieth century to prove this assertion. There may come a day in the near future, however, when we will realize that the Christian answer to the problem of community is the only effective alternative to communism. And from the Christian point of view education is one important facet of this overall community problem. Possibly the recovery of spiritual vitality waits for the "whole" household of Christian faith in the community to discover a practical medium in which it can totally relate itself to the education of the whole community.

But if the local community is chosen as the setting for initial steps in the removal of some of the tensions between great divisions of Christian faith as they relate to education, we must seriously re-examine two traditional concepts which today defer all but the remotest hopes for success. The first of these traditions is the principle of the separation of church and state, or more specifically in this instance, the separation of Christian faith from public education. The second tradition is the Roman Catholic policy of separatism in relation to education in the community. One could hardly expect, however, that these two principles, solidly entrenched in the histories of Protestantism and Catholicism, should easily submit to modification unless an increasing area of reciprocal trust gradually emerges from the past generations of conflict and distrust. It seems at least possible, however, to move toward a closer understanding as twentieth century urgencies are faced by both factions in their attempt to relate themselves constructively to education in the local community. In any event there are some important essentials about which Reformation faith and Catholic faith agree in principle and which offer a common starting point.

In the first place, both Reformation faith and Catholic faith agree that education is a family function (or an extension of the family function) and not primarily a state function. Emil Brunner, for example, argues that even for the state schools the state should not educate, but should provide the framework for the cultural direction of the educative process. An inward separation between the state and education is necessary. Maritain, the Catholic philosopher, agrees by saying that the state should provide the fullest plural expression of the cultural activities of the body politic, and this pluralistic expression of the people (including education, we presume) is a movement from the bottom upward. Since both Roman Catholic faith and Reformation faith conceive of the democratic state as the arm of the people which arbitrates and administers justice rather than participates in the cultural life of the people, it seems logical that the local community is the key group within which the cultural problem of acknowledging God in education ought to be realistically faced.

Reformation faith points to the educational ideals of Pestalozzi, who believed that the home was the foundation of education and that the larger education of the community was an extension of that which was begun in the home. The Catholic outlook, too, stresses the importance of the family to education. The Catholic sacrament of marriage immeasurably accents the church's regard for the educational responsibilities of the home. Education is inseparable from the holy order of family existence.

If this federalistic principle is primary to a vital community education, especially as it is faced with the problem of developing responsible persons, the whole question of the relationship of the state to education needs a critical reexamination. If the family-of-families educational framework is the essential starting point for education in the community and if the vigor of such an education must accumulate from the grass roots upward, not only should there be a separation between ecclesiastical organizations and education, but also an inward separation between the state and local public education. Emil Brunner points out that the Enlightenment separated the schools from the organized church. Now perhaps it is time for a new enlightenment which suggests the protection of the local school function from the growing dominance of the state as it threatens to overstep its bounds as arbiter in educational matters. The local community, generally composed of many faiths, undoubtedly will not submit to an organizational church imposition, but the community ought to be equally aware of the danger of collectivism, which in the end could be as much or more devastating. These secular forms of centralism presently overshadowing the education within the local communities are a danger against which both Reformation faith and Roman Catholic faith ought to be commonly opposed.

The state, according to this generally conservative Christian view, can best relate itself to public education as an overseer in the name of justice based on reason. J. S. Mill's essay *On Liberty* presents a concise view on the matter; the state, wrote Mills, should enforce education for all, but parents ought to be free to decide how and where. And Christian faith would add that the community should not only decide "how" and "where," but also "what."

In the second place Catholicism and Reformation Christian faith are drawing closer together in their understanding of the permeative relationship of Christian faith to the education of the community. Because Protestantism is historically separated from education, it has placed strong emphasis upon the principle of general spiritual permeation rather than direct organizational influence. But Maritain also speaks of the leaven of Christian faith as the church's "superior strength of all-pervading inspiration."[1] The end of the state is the over-all protection and promotion of the culture (which ought to be a Christian culture), and the church is accountable for the immediate task of spiritually enlivening the community. The more completely a people are imbued with Christian convictions, the more effectively they will strengthen all components of the body politic, including the state itself. The leaven of the Gospel sets free the natural accumulation of human inclinations which evolve into higher and higher concepts of the natural law, and the natural law constitutes a religiously undergirded but rationally out-

[1] Jacques Maritain, *Man and the State* (Chicago, 1951), 162.

linable means for ordering the cultural activities of the community. It is obvious, says Maritain, that the church cannot proceed today as it did in the Middle Ages, because the present church lives in a secular world and there is no hope for a definite ecclesiastical control over the whole of culture. Permeation, therefore, is to be accented, while an insistence on the principle of uncompromising ecclesiastical suzerainty needs to be held somewhat in abeyance.

A recent statement by Pope Pius XII further indicates a significant trend toward moderation on the part of the Catholic Church in its relation to cultural problems. A papal voice for tolerance address, December 6, 1953, pointed out that God has not given even human authority "an absolute and universal command in matters of faith and morality." There is a higher norm which permits in some cases the "toleration of error in order to promote the greater good."[2] Even though the Catholic Church may remain uncompromising in its theological formulations, it does often show a remarkable flexibility in practical matters. Because the Catholic Church subscribes to the idea of a necessary cultural development through family and community upward, the time may come when this church will decide that the problem of "community" is urgent enough to warrant its co-operative support of at least one segment of community education in order to bolster the general defenses of Christendom against nontheological secularism.

In the third place both Catholic and Reformation faiths propose that Christian faith should relate itself in a positive way to its cultural surroundings, although these proposals are based upon somewhat different philosophical and theological bases.

Roman Catholic faith, in comparison to modern Protestantism, undoubtedly has a well-balanced philosophical formula for determining the relationship of the church to the

2 Quoted by M. Searle Bates, "Crisis in Catholic Columbia," in *The Christian Century*, LXXI (1954), 786-88.

world, and this formula also covers the question of the relationship of the church to education. The life of man belongs to two worlds, and God has created him to participate meaningfully in both. Man exercises his God-given reason in his work in the temporal community, and through faith the church is able to restore man's deprived spiritual nature, enabling him to be a citizen in the eternal kingdom as well as fulfilling his capacity to work toward the good life on earth.

By contrast, Protestantism is more easily beset with unfortunate extremes as it tries to discover the right relationship between the church and the world, and the Christian's participation in either or both. Some forms of Protestantism assume that the world is hopelessly evil and that Christians should separate themselves from the world as completely as possible. Other modern expressions of Protestantism tend toward an opposite extreme and assume that the church is hardly more than a natural cultural product like other worldly institutions and that it is not essentially different from the world. (Of course the Christian church from the beginning has struggled with this problem, and its answers have varied significantly with the particular historical settings.) Neo-Reformation Christian faith tries to solve this problem in the light of the Biblical dictum that Christians are in the world but not of it. A Christian is a person spiritually renewed, and in this respect he is separate from the spirit of the world; but a Christian is nevertheless in the world, and it is his responsibility to participate constructively in the cultural life of the community in which he lives.

The Catholic man with his two-storied nature—his rational nature and his ecclesiastically restored supernature— is free to participate in the temporal cultural activities without violating his first responsibility to God and the church. The Catholic believer has an outstanding advantage of solving the problem of citizenship in two worlds, because theo-

retically there need not be any serious tension between his
loyalty to the world, which may be his rational response,
and his loyalty to the church, which is his response by faith.
Man's temporal responsibilities and loyalties are quite clearly
distinguished from his ecclesiastical and theological loyalties,
but they are not theoretically contradictory, because rational
activity in the world guided by natural law is not contradictory to higher spiritual truth discovered in the church.
Of course ecclesiastical loyalty must always stand over temporal loyalty if there is any area of conflict.

For Reformation faith the problem is not as simply worked
out. Man is not essentially a two-storied creature but a single
being who as a person is totally related to both God and the
world. It is difficult in such a case to divide one's loyalties
between two worlds when the temporal world is considered
radically different from the eternal kingdom of God. Reformation faith therefore tends to place the Christian in a
paradoxical position. A Christian belongs wholly to the
kingdom of God, but he must do with all his might the
thing that his hand finds to do in the world where he presently lives. Yet it seems that in spite of a different approach
to the problem, both the Catholic Christian and the Reformation Christian are committed to respond in a positive
way to the cultural demands of their communities.

These bases for practical agreement about cultural "federalism," spiritual permeation, and the necessity for a positive Christian response to the needs of the community are
counterbalanced by at least one overwhelming fundamental
disagreement between Protestant and Catholic faiths as they
relate to education, and of course this is the problem of
authority. A great gulf of separation is involved in the
question of the authoritative relationship of the church to
the whole community, of which the church is a part. For
practical purposes any community needs a final authority
to which it turns for the proper ordering of its cultural

activities. The Roman Catholic Church uncompromisingly insists that it is the highest tribunal and that it must make authoritative decisions about moral aspects of the cultural functions (which include education) of the community. This position of the church does not propose to interfere with the democratic functioning of government. Government is a rational function, and its structure should be supported democratically from the bottom upward. Persons who rule authoritatively should be given this privilege by the people. But the rational activity of government has to do primarily with arbitration and the administration of justice between the many groups and interests of the community. And this rational function of the government derived from the people is not sovereign within itself but is conditioned by a Higher Sovereignty. The church, because it is the representative of this Higher Sovereignty, stands above the functions of government as well as the cultural activities of the people. The church makes known God's will for the eternal spiritual destiny of men, and it possesses an authority which moves from above downward by virtue of God's revelation. Governmental authorities are genuinely the vicars of the people under God and rightfully exercise temporal authority, but the final church authority is represented in the Pope, the vicar of God. Education is a cultural function and should be subject to the rational administration and authority of the vicars of the people insofar as justice is concerned, but it is reserved for the church to determine the content and the purposes of all education, because education is inseparably connected with the eternal spiritual life of man and not his temporal existence only. And the church as the body of Christ speaks with unquestioned authority on these vital matters in education.

Reformation faith takes exception to this definition of the final authority of the Roman Catholic Church in relation to the cultural activities of the whole community. The church, instead of being a "sinless organization of sinful men," is an organization which in spite of its supernatural character is also subject to the sinful perversions of all humanity. To invest final authority in any organization, including the church, is exceedingly dangerous to the body politic.

For Reformation faith, final authority for the community can most safely be vested in the people. And one of the tasks of Reformation Christian faith is to develop a genuine sense of responsibility in the hearts of as many people as possible so that the authoritative voice of the people can most effectively represent the voice and authority of the eternal God. The people, of course, are not sovereign but stand under the sovereign God. When the people lose their faith in God, their democratic authority loses its validity and the culture suffers accordingly. The only hope for a continuing good authority is that the people, or at least as large a majority of them as possible, personally acknowledge God as their ultimate Authority, and the authority of the people tends to be good or bad according to the extent of loyalty of the people to God, who is sovereign over all. Thus the relationship of the church to education, according to Reformation faith, is primarily indirect and permeative. Yet interest in education is vital and direct because, under-girded by godly faith, it is an important means toward developing responsible citizens not only for their personal advantage, but also for the community advantage, for such citizens provide the best means toward a just authority.

The Protestant concept of authority is based upon the will of the people under God. But the church, in this view, ought not organizationally to attempt to regulate the organizational framework of the community. The church's task is primarily spiritual and personal, a work of faith. The organizational framework of the community or the state as a whole is primarily a rational and impersonal activity.

The church ought not to regulate cultural activities organizationally, but should refer this task to the state or the community. The church indeed stands above the state and the culture, but the relationship is permeative. To the degree that a community is Christian, the church stands above every person in a personal and "faith" relationship, while in turn every person stands above the cultural functions of the community by virtue of his share in democratic authority and also by his personal influence. The church does not regulate and control as "the church"; if so, it usurps the place of the state. Rather the church stands above and behind each of its members in the community, and each member as a citizen contributes to the formation of the final authority for the community insofar as regulation and control are concerned.

This basic schism between Protestant faith and its derivative, the American form of government, on the one hand, and Catholic faith with its essentially nondemocratic authoritarianism on the other hand, leads to an unfortunate state of affairs in the educational activities of the community. In the first instance, a member of the Catholic Church supposedly has a unique philosophical and theological heritage which ought to enable him to solve the problem of participating influentially in the world and at the same time being a member of the kingdom of God. Yet his church's inflexible view on its authority, even about the general cultural activities of the community, separates the Catholic from his community at a critical point, so that the education of the children of the community is broken up into discrete uncommunicative compartments.

For different reasons Protestantism, too, is paradoxically separated from the educational functions of the community. The traditional Protestant principle of separation of the churches from the schools makes it impractical for Protestant faith to relate itself in any effective practical manner to community education, even though Reformation faith is definitely committed to the proposition that the church and Christians individually should relate themselves effectively to their communities for the sake of the kingdom of God. Protestantism historically has so vigorously protected education against unacceptable faiths that it has quite successfully shielded public education even from its own Christian influences.

Both of these forms of Christian separatism testify to serious weaknesses in Christian faith in its ability to address itself effectively to the community in distress. Somewhere in the vicious circle of check and countercheck within Christendom itself there ought to be a means of diminishing the intensity of this division as it relates to education. What are some of the possible courses of action?

First of all let us consider again the Catholic position of separatism in education. The fundamental Catholic doctrine that man is a member of two worlds ought to be amenable to revision in its application to practical problems. And possibly a revision without violating the basic principle must turn on the question of withdrawal and return: At what point must faith and the church stand without compromise, and where may faith and the church share certain responsibilities co-operatively with the whole community of which the church is a part? Education, for example, is a term which covers a tremendous scope of activity. The principle of withdrawal would not necessarily need to apply to the whole field of education, especially when the principle of return in some levels of education could conceivably reap rich dividends for all concerned.

The whole question of withdrawal is historically significant for the church, and currently as much as ever a crucial problem for Christian faith. This tendency toward withdrawal always seems definitely in evidence where the traditional forms of the Christian faith are adhered to, whether

Protestant or Catholic, and this bent on the part of the Christian church cannot be taken lightly in the face of Biblical teachings and church history. Note, for example, this theme of separatism in the history of the Jewish people, as well as in New Testament faith. John Bright in his book *The Kingdom of God* carefully outlines the evidence of a minority acting in the capacity of a suffering servant which separates itself from the world at large and commits itself to the spiritual redemption of the whole. Today the Roman Catholic Church without question develops great spiritual force through its various practices of withdrawal and sacrificial commitment. Likewise, in certain Protestant groups this separatist tendency is strong, and their practice of withdrawal gives them a spiritual power which the world seems not to know of.

It would seem that the Christian principle of withdrawal ought not to be challenged but simply recognized as a means toward great spiritual strength. Rather, the significant question to be raised is this: Where should "withdrawal" be emphasized, and where should "return" be considered? These days, more than ever, all persons in the community seem inevitably thrown into juxtaposition one way or another, although this growing trend toward more intricate interrelationships does not necessarily indicate greater genuine community. Christians have no choice but to share on a cultural plane the spiritual ebbs and flows of their community. Today it seems more difficult than ever for any man to build a wall around himself or his family to shield against unacceptable inroads of community influence. Because of this inescapable cultural impact, often unfavorable, the church faces a distressing problem. Is education, or at least certain levels of education, necessarily the point at which the church should insist on withdrawal, when the primary purpose of withdrawal on the educational level is much compromised at every turn due to the nature of the modern community? Education only partly occurs in the schoolroom, while much vital education takes place outside the bounds of the formal process. When, therefore, withdrawal appears far from being effective on the practical educational level, is there not at least one area of education which might be considered a point of "return" by the church, with a view toward the spiritual improvement of the whole community?

Possibly a reasonable suggestion, to some extent not far removed from the teachings of Catholic philosopher Maritain, implies not a lessening of the principle of withdrawal but a shift of emphasis. It would seem not at all intemperate or un-Catholic to center the church's emphasis upon "withdrawal" in the stricter confines of the religious community— the body of believers. Surely this is an area of freedom infinitely important to free men, that they be free to worship with whom they choose in the manner which they choose and that they be not unnecessarily entangled with the cultural or secular demands of the temporal community with its ever present disruptive spiritual influences. The church community of believers through its freedom of withdrawal generates a spiritual power which purifies the community. Where education lies closest to this spiritual ministration of the church, that is, education in the family and education of the very young, it should seemingly come under the jurisdiction of the church. Likewise, higher education seems to be intimately related to the spiritual aims of the church, and historically the relationship between the church and higher education has undoubtedly proved itself outstanding. But for the sake of the unity and the necessary integration of the whole community of which all members share in the common but precious experience of living in freedom, there ought to be a level of education where all meet and all avenues are open for the freer interpenetration of spiritual vitality into the body politic. This procedure might be the beginning step in providing a Christian alternative to some form of secular collectivism which is formed from outward pressure and not through inward spiritual strength.

Of course public education cannot continue to deteriorate without forcing Christian groups to withdraw for sheer protection of their young against the debilitating influences of low morale. But this withdrawal can hardly be considered more than a temporary expedient. Both Catholic faith and Reformation faith are committed to an aggressive permeation and renewal of the community. Somehow the concept of salvation by "withdrawal" without "return" seems inconsistent with the spirit of Christian faith. This idea is reminiscent of the story of some adventurers lost in an Alaskan blizzard. One of the men deserted a comrade who had fallen in the snow, assuming that he must save himself. The other man decided to lose his life if necessary helping the fallen man to safety. The first man eventually lost his strength and fell to die alone in the snow. The second man carrying his human burden was warmed by the life of his fellow human being, and both eventually reached shelter. Christian faith invariably counteracts the concept of withdrawal alone with the pronouncement that man cannot live unto himself alone. Christian faith in America still enjoys virtually unlimited opportunity for withdrawal in its life of the spirit where it can work hard at keeping the church pure and holy and spiritually strong. But Christian faith needs also the spiritual exercise involved in the return to the life of the community at large, and education is one of these critical areas where "return" is a vital protective principle as well as the idea of "withdrawal" for spiritual protection. By withdrawal the church protects its own sensitive area from the corruption of the world, but also by the same token it withdraws itself from the opportunity to serve the community in a spiritually receptive area.

While any serious integration of Catholic and Reformation theology seems impossible at this point, the time is never too late to take seriously even the slightest shifts toward integration on the practical level. Obviously no kind of overnight solution is in sight for this whole complex problem. But at least some movement toward a tolerable solution seems terribly necessary as an alternative to cultural disintegration in the community. While the principle of withdrawal is assumed to be a necessary and valuable part of the history of Christian faith, it should also be noted that the fragmentation of the free community into unsocial, jealous, and tiny alien sovereignties is the beginning of the end of what has been taken for granted as the community of free persons. Although the freedom for withdrawal ought to be essential to free society, there must also be taken into account the element of accountability for responsible associations between all groups in the community. These responsible associations must be taken into account simply because they cannot be avoided by the members of any community. An artificial separation of American citizens on the practical level in the community can easily degenerate into a case of irresponsibility. Responsibility surely implies responsiveness to one's neighbor. If a certain degree of practical responsibility does not exist between Christian groups in the local community, the possibilities for any positive and vigorous promotion of the whole principle of responsibility in education seems seriously handicapped indeed.

The practical level for the promotion of responsible relationships in the community through education should be able to find its common ground in "reason," if no other. Reason ought to conclude that the various proponents of Christian faith should be commonly engaged in the spiritual support of public education, that there can be an educational meeting ground based upon the common essentials of Christian faith. It is true that faith is basic in the Christian concept of personal salvation as well as in the communion of the saints, the body of believers, the church; in

areas of withdrawal the faith element ought to be the decisive factor. But Christian faith is also vitally concerned
with areas of return to the world, and in these working
areas reason must be acknowledged its important assignment.
Reason becomes significant on the practical level because
work must be done on a co-operative basis involving many
variations of faith. Faith working with faith often is not
practical, because men, being sinful and turned aside with
error and pride, do not have perfect faiths. Imperfect faiths
find it difficult to engage on common ground, because faiths
of any kind are the response of the whole person in absolute
terms characterized by the principle of certainty. Thus,
varying faiths exercised by imperfect and sinful persons can
hardly be compromised. But reason operating in terms of
law discovers a tolerable existence for persons in community.
If faith were perfect, community would be perfect; but faith
is not perfect, and reason underwritten by faith provides a
working solution. This work of reason Christian faith ought
to recognize. The law is man's practical answer to sinful
fragmentative human existence, though not a Christian answer to man's eternal salvation. Although faith stands above
reason, there should not be any Christian inhibition against
the use of reason to solve temporal community problems,
even such spiritual problems as the necessity for acknowledging God in education. Surely modern Protestantism is
not so much a stranger to reason that its faith must preclude
an appeal to reason for practical considerations. Likewise,
Thomism holds itself eminently qualified to participate on
a rational basis in the solution of temporal problems which
beset the local community.

The second traditional bulwark, which ought to be re-
considered from the Protestant point of view particularly,
is the principle of church and state separation. This principle applies to education at two critical points: first, that
the state ought not materially to support any sectarian pro-

The Community and Christian Faith

gram of education, and second, that public education ought not to promote any sectarian religious emphasis. This discussion assumes that the first statement referring to the public support of sectarian educational institutions ought not to be subjected to any substantial changes. Sectarian religious groups ought to be free to promote their own preferred type of education without expectation of public assistance. This principle is a safeguard to both the state and to the private institution. Material support ought never to be allowed to confuse and to attenuate the worthy spiritual purposes which can be most effectively worked out when private education remains free from political entanglements and the associated pecuniary temptations. Furthermore, if the Roman Catholic Church should ever see its way clear to participate in at least a part of the total community educative program, this first aspect of the problem of church and state separation would be somewhat minimized. The Catholic Church then would no longer bear so heavy a financial burden educationally, as is now the case with its double assignment to support both parochial and public education.

The primary concern here is the area of public education and its more effective relationships to Christian faith in general. The law as it now stands, along with notable decisions of the Supreme Court, appears obsolescent and uncognizant of the deeper issues of the relationships of faith to education. Along with shifts from theological to relativistic foundations in all fields of knowledge, it seems that the law, too, shifted from its traditional religious foundations to a pragmatic basis, the relativistic nature of which does not give proper insight into the relation between faith and reason. Recent court decisions have not seemed fully to recognize the fact that neutrality is no longer possible, even for reason, or for education, or for law itself. But today there appears a lively hope for a counter trend in this respect, possibly foreshadowed by the recent decision to insert "under

God" in the pledge to the flag. If a real possibility exists for a growing recognition of God in the state, a real possibility exists also for the modification of federal laws to make possible the freer interaction between Christian faith and public education.

The relaxation of the obsolescent and artificial blockage which exists between faith and education is essential not only to Roman Catholic faith but also to Protestant faiths. In the first place, earlier sectarian theological conflicts are not nearly so disruptive today as they were a century ago. Now a new danger more serious than sectarian conflict has appeared on the educational scene, and that danger is non-theological secularism which is apparently uninhibited by law and tradition to manifest its influences in the public school program. While a Protestant majority keeps Catholicism out of the public schools, it also provides the lawful shield for secular faiths to work uninhibited by law.

One of the primary revisions in this problem of church and state separation ought to be a re-evaluation of the proper relationship of the individual to the prevailing faith of the community. A single person, or even a small minority, ought not to be able to subvert an attempt by the community to undergird a program of education with basic Christian principles simply because he does not subscribe to them. Of course Christian faith ought to be devoted to the tenet that individuals and groups must always be free to withdraw from the majority in order to carry out their religious and educational responsibilities according to the dictates of their consciences and within the confines of reason as designated by the state. And obviously no religion must ever be arbitrarily forced upon the conscience of any man. But on the other hand the community, too, ought to have its rights, one of them being the reasonable means of constructively basing its education upon the Christian heritage of the Western world if it sees fit to do so, this to be accomplished free from the legal interference by either an individual or a minority that chooses not to accept this traditional Christian heritage. The day of supposed neutrality is gone for the Western world. The supposed rational conclusion that the state or education or the law or that any man can be neutral about faith is not a rational conclusion at all. And as long as Christendom nominally constitutes the majority of most communities in America, it ought to act while there is yet time to restore the leaven of Christian faith at practical levels in the cultural activities of the community. Yet where a Christian majority exists and claims a right to support education with Christian faith, it must at the same time remember the rational assumption that any person and any minority must be free to withdraw according to the dictates of conscience.

The actual working out of this freer support of public education by Christian faith ought primarily to be a community affair. In many communities this development will be positive and effective, while in other communities this movement may be negative if little vital Christian faith exists. But in any event the whole principle of church and state separation ought in some way to be relaxed in order to allow greater freedom for community decision about these matters. Communities should be less hampered in the use of their own ingenious and flexible proposals for the solutions of their problems relating to faith and education. Let the state continue to supervise and maintain justice when necessary in local educational matters and in the protection of individual conscience, but also let Christian faith work out suitable community solutions where it has the will and the initiative to do so. And let the various segments of Christian faith in the community formulate their practical procedures in terms of reason, undergirded and supported by faith. Let communities work at the problem of spiritual permeation, on the one hand, and let them, on the other hand, work at the establishment of their own safeguards against untoward ecclesiastical violations of justice and reason.

These suggestions should hardly be evaluated against some backdrop of perfectionism or utopianism. We live in a sinful world, and each generation must endure its travail in attempting to establish a tolerable state of affairs. This work, if it works at all, must necessarily be sponsored by Christian realists rather than by anxious advocates of perfectibility who insist upon all or nothing. The practical effort toward a stabler framework in the community seems urgently necessary to avert the present danger of fragmentation of communities and faiths. Of course integration should not (nor can it be) forced. If communities do not choose to reason about these matters and to commit themselves to an integrative course, tragedy seems the likely alternative.

Education is a cultural activity as it deals with the tasks of learning arithmetic, history, geography, the social sciences, and so on, but these activities require a "faith" setting. Our communities with their Christian heritage need the faith which is inseparable from that heritage. But Christian faith, if it hopes to provide bases for the solution of the problem of responsibility in the education of the community, must first apply its eternal wisdom toward its own responsible conduct in the community. No immovable obstruction really stands in the way of practical Christian co-operation, other than the perversity and pride of human nature itself—and Christian faith has been responsibly entrusted with the eternal means to overcome these human impediments.

Critical Essay on References

GENERAL REFERENCES

A GENERAL background study for the problems with which this treatise is concerned commits one to an assignment which is never completed—a reading program which insures at least a beginning acquaintanceship with the classical writings of the Western world. A great number of books are helpful in introducing the student to these basic writings. John H. Randall's *The Making of the Modern Mind* (Boston, 1940) is a stimulating and scholarly survey of Western thought and its relationship to the present. Others are Ralph H. Gabriel, *The Course of American Democratic Thought* (New York, 1940); Nicolai Hartmann, *Ethics* (3 vols., New York, 1932); George H. Sabine, *A History of Political Theory* (New York, 1937); Preserved Smith, *A History of Modern Culture* (2 vols., New York, 1930); Arnold J. Toynbee, *A Study of History*, abridged by D. C. Somervell (New York, 1947); Frederick Copleston, *A History of Philosophy* (Westminster, Md., 1950), Vol. II; W. G. Muelder and Laurence Sears (eds.), *The Development of American Philosophy* (Boston, 1940); W. H. Werkmeister, *A History of Philosophical Ideas in America* (New York, 1949); William K. Wright, *A History of Modern Philosophy* (New York, 1941); Bertrand Russell, *A History of Western Philosophy* (New York, 1945); Edgar Brightman, *An Introduction to Philosophy* (New York, 1925); and Maurice de Wulf, *Philosophy and Civilization in the Middle Ages* (Princeton, 1922).

These books are a few of the references which provide a stimulus for reading the basic works of some of the classic philosophers and theologians, such as Plato and Aristotle, Augustine, Aquinas, and Calvin, the writings of whom are all significantly related to the current problems in education as elaborated in this book.

General references in education which provide valuable background material are John S. Brubacher, *Modern Philosophies of Education* (2nd ed., New York, 1950); J. Donald Butler, *Four*

Philosophies and Their Practice in Education and Religion (New York, 1951); National Society for the Study of Education, 41st Yearbook, *Philosophies of Education,* Part I (Chicago, 1942); and Robert Ulich (ed.), *Three Thousand Years of Educational Wisdom* (Cambridge, Mass., 1948).

PROGRESSIVISM

Books

JOHN Dewey's *Democracy and Education* (New York, 1916) is often called the bible of progressivism. This book, although written almost forty years ago, continues to be outstanding in comparison to much of the subsequent literature on modern education. John Dewey was an unusually prolific writer. Out of the scores of other publications these books are suggested as an outline of his philosophy in general: *The Quest for Certainty* (New York, 1929), *Logic: The Theory of Inquiry* (New York, 1938), *Reconstruction in Philosophy* (New York, 1920), *Human Nature and Conduct* (New York, 1922), *Ethics,* with James H. Tufts (New York, 1908), *Interest and Effort in Education* (Boston, 1913), and *A Common Faith* (New Haven, 1934).

William Heard Kilpatrick is probably Dewey's most distinguished disciple, a kind of mediator between Dewey's theory and educational practice. The outline of Kilpatrick's educational views is neatly summarized in his latest book, *Philosophy of Education* (New York, 1951). William Clayton Bower, a progressive in the theological field, has lately been somewhat of a philosophical father to progressivism in action on the moral level in education, particularly in the experiment of the Kentucky moral and spiritual values movement. In connection with this movement William Clayton Bower has written *Moral and Spiritual Values in Education* (Lexington, Ky., 1952). *Character through Creative Experience* (Chicago, 1930) provides a helpful background study to Dr. Bower's current educational views. John L. Childs is also an important contributor to the liberal emphasis in education, and possibly his most important book is *Education and Morals* (New York, 1950).

By all means we should not neglect to mention William James. His books, *Pragmatism* (New York, 1907) and *Essays on Radical*

Empiricism (New York, 1922), provide an important philosophical foundation for the twentieth century emphasis on progressive education.

Other important references to the progressive point of view in education include Alfred S. Clayton, *Emergent Mind and Education* (New York, 1943); George S. Counts, *Dare the School Build a New Social Order* (New York, 1932); Education Policies Commission, *Learning the Ways of Democracy* (Washington, 1940); George Mead, *Mind, Self, and Society* (Chicago, 1934); James Mursell, *Education for American Democracy* (New York, 1943); Harold Rugg, *Foundations for American Education* (Yonkers-on-Hudson, N. Y., 1947); B. Othanel Smith, William O. Stanley, and J. Harlan Shores, *Fundamentals of Curriculum Development* (Yonkers-on-Hudson, N. Y., 1950).

Articles

Progressive Education (1924-   ), published in New York by the American Education Fellowship, *The Social Frontier* (1934-1943), published by Columbia University, and *Educational Theory* (1951-   ), published at the University of Illinois, are three periodicals notable for their commitment to the progressive point of view in education. "Academic Freedom and Responsibility," an editorial in *The Social Frontier,* II (1936), 191-92, is significant in its view on the problem of responsibility in education. These articles are also helpful: William Heard Kilpatrick, "Moral Freedom and Scientific Determinism," in *Educational Theory,* II (1952), 11-19; Victor Yarros, "Toward the American Commonwealth," in *The Social Frontier,* V (1938), 89-90.

Two important articles written by John Dewey are, "Evolution and Ethics," in *The Monist,* VIII (1898), 321-41, and "The Evolutionary Methods as Applied to Morality," in *The Philosophical Review,* XI (1902), 107-24.

Bulletins and Reports

A series of bulletins were published by the Kentucky State Department of Education on the moral and spiritual values program of that state. The bulletin entitled *Moral and Spiritual Values in Education* (Frankfort, 1950) is an informative report on the Kentucky program and its basic philosophy; *Moral and Spiritual Values in the Public Schools* (Frankfort, 1952), published by the same department, gives a digest of the summer school lectures of William Heard Kilpatrick at the University of Kentucky.

The Educational Policies Commission has published materials relating to the moral problems of education, for example, *Moral and Spiritual Values in the Public Schools* (Washington, 1951).

CLASSICAL HUMANISM

Books

ROBERT M. Hutchins and Mortimer Adler are two of the most spectacular defenders of the classical view in current educational circles today. Neither of these educators does an unusual amount of writing, although Adler is widely known for his *How to Read a Book* (New York, 1940), and three or four of Hutchins' publications are well known, including *Education for Freedom* (Baton Rouge, 1943), *The Education We Need* (Chicago, 1947), *The Higher Learning in America* (New Haven, 1936), and recently, *Conflict in Education in a Democratic Society* (New York, 1953). Mortimer Adler wrote a series of articles which demonstrate the Aristotelian dialectic applied to the current threat of moral relativism. See below under "Articles."

Other important books which relate to this section are: Bernard Iddings Bell, *Crisis in Education* (New York, 1949); Ernst Cassirer, *An Essay on Man* (New Haven, 1944); Norman Foerster (ed.), *Humanism and America* (New York, 1930), and *The Future of the Liberal College* (New York, 1938). Werner Jaeger is an outstanding authority on early Greek education; his noteworthy work in this respect is *Paideia* (3 vols., New York, 1945). I. L. Kandel has written a book which critically examines modern progressivism, entitled *The Cult of Uncertainty* (New York, 1943).

These works, too, are helpful references: Richard W. Livingstone, *Greek Ideals and Modern Life* (London, 1935), and *Some Tasks for Education* (London, 1946); Jacques Maritain, *Education at the Crossroads* (New Haven, 1943); Everett D. Martin, *The Meaning of a Liberal Education* (New York, 1926); Louis

J. Mercier, *The Challenge of Humanism* (New York, 1936); Walter Moberly, *The Crisis in the University* (London, 1951); Paul E. More, *On Being Human* (Princeton, 1936); Arnold S. Nash, *The University and the Modern World* (New York, 1944); Jose y Gassett Ortega, *Mission of the University* (Princeton, 1944); Karl R. Popper, *The Open Society and Its Enemies* (2 vols., London, 1945); Mark Van Doren, *Liberal Education* (New York, 1943); Alfred N. Whitehead, *The Aims of Education* (New York, 1929); Irving Babbitt, *Democracy and Leadership* (Boston, 1924); Albert Lynd, *Quackery in the Public Schools* (Boston, 1953); Gilbert Highet, *Man's Unconquered Mind* (New York, 1954); Arthur E. Bestor, *Educational Wastelands: The Retreat from Learning in Our Public Schools* (Urbana, 1953).

Articles

Mortimer Adler applies the method of classical philosophy, particularly Aristotelianism, to the moral problem in "A Dialectic of Morals," in *The Review of Politics*, III (1941), 3-31, 188-224, 350-94. A summary of Adler's philosophy can be found in the article "Liberalism and Liberal Education," in *The Educational Record*, XX (1939), 422-36.

T. S. Eliot has written an outstanding series of articles entitled "The Aims of Education," in *Measure*, II (1950-1951), 1-16, 191-203, 285-97, 362-75.

Bulletins and Reports

Two excellent bulletins deal with the classical point of view in modern education. The first is the report of the Harvard Committee, *General Education in a Free Society* (Cambridge, 1945), and the second is the Forty-First Yearbook of the National Society for the Study of Education, *Philosophies of Education*, Part I (Chicago, 1942), particularly the section written by Mortimer Adler.

EDUCATIONAL RECONSTRUCTIONISM

Books

THE TRANSITION in education from the progressive and usually moderate pragmatic emphasis to the more radical views of the educational reconstructionists is often difficult to trace clearly.

Beginning with the earlier and milder revolutionaries in the progressivist ranks, and moving toward the current and more radical philosophers and sociologists, educational and otherwise, this list of authors is suggested: George S. Counts, *Dare the School Build a New Social Order* (New York, 1932); John L. Childs, *Education and the Philosophy of Experimentalism* (New York, 1931); Sidney Hook, *From Hegel to Marx* (New York, 1936), and *John Dewey* (New York, 1939); Harold Rugg, *Foundations for American Education* (Yonkers-on-Hudson, N. Y., 1947); Harry Slochower, *No Voice Is Wholly Lost* (New York, 1945); B. Othanel Smith, William O. Stanley, and J. Harlan Shores, *Fundamentals of Curriculum Development* (Yonkers-on-Hudson, N. Y., 1950); Alexander Meiklejohn, *Education between Two Worlds* (New York, 1942); Harold Laski, *The American Democracy* (New York, 1948); Karl Mannheim, *Man and Society in an Age of Reconstruction* (New York, 1941); Kurt Lewin, *Field Theory in Social Science* (New York, 1951); and *Resolving Social Conflicts* (New York, 1948).

Studies of Rousseau provide important background for this section, as, for example, *The Living Thoughts of Rousseau,* ed. by Romain Rolland (New York, 1939); *The Social Contract;* and *Emile.*

Possibly today the outstanding writer on the reconstructionist theme in education is Theodore Brameld. Brameld's main work is *Patterns of Educational Philosophy: A Democratic Interpretation* (Yonkers-on-Hudson, N. Y., 1950). Other books by Brameld are *Design for America* (New York, 1945) and *Minority Problems in the Public Schools* (New York, 1946). *Education and Morals* (New York, 1950), by John L. Childs, is also one of the important recent publications which illustrates a somewhat more unapologetic secular support of important reconstructionist principles than seems to be discoverable in the earlier moderate progressivism of the pragmatists of a few decades ago.

Articles

Harold Laski, noted English socialist, was one of the contributors to *The Social Frontier,* the editorial policy of which reveals an unmistakable leftward swing in contrast to earlier pragmatic views. "A New Education Needs a New World," in

The Social Frontier, II (1936), 144-47, by Laski, is representative of this trend. Frank C. Wegener has written a critical article entitled "The 'Ontology' of Reconstructionism," in *Educational Theory,* II (1952), 45-47.

EDUCATION, THE COMMUNITY, AND CHRISTIAN FAITH

Books

IN THE formulation of the Neo-Reformation outlook, Emil Brunner is considered one of the key theologians. Brunner's most important works insofar as this book is concerned are *Man in Revolt* (Philadelphia, 1947), *The Divine Imperative* (Philadelphia, 1947), *Christianity and Civilization* (2 vols., New York, 1948-1949), *Justice and the Social Order* (New York, 1945), and *The Church in the New Social Order* (London, 1952).

Reinhold Niebuhr is also considered an eminent authority in this field. His outstanding work in this connection is *The Nature and Destiny of Man* (2 vols., New York, 1941-1943). Other valuable Niebuhr books are *Moral Man and Immoral Society* (New York, 1946), *Christianity and Power Politics* (New York, 1946), *The Children of Light and the Children of Darkness* (New York, 1945), and *The Irony of American History* (New York, 1952).

Other helpful works include John Baillie, *An Invitation to Pilgrimage* (New York, 1942), and *Our Knowledge of God* (New York, 1939); Nicolas Berdyaev, *The Destiny of Man* (London, 1945), *The Meaning of History* (London, 1949), and *Slavery and Freedom* (New York, 1944); Martin Buber, *Between Man and Man* (New York, 1948); John Calvin, *Institutes of the Christian Religion;* St. Augustine, *Confessions* and *The City of God;* T. S. Eliot, *Essays Ancient and Modern* (London, 1947), and *Notes toward the Definition of Culture* (New York, 1949); T. E. Jessop and others, *The Christian Understanding of Man* (London, 1938); S. S. Laurie, *John Amos Comenius* (Cambridge, Eng., 1893); C. S. Lewis, *The Abolition of Man* (New York, 1947); *Malvern, 1941: The Life of the Church and the Order of Society* (London, 1941); Wilhelm Pauck, *The Heritage of the Reformation* (Boston, 1950); Johann Pestalozzi, *Leonard and Gertrude;* Paul Tillich, *The Protestant Era* (Chicago, 1948); Henry P. Van

206   Essay on References

Dusen, *God in Education* (New York, 1951); George A. Buttrick, *Faith and Education* (New York, 1952); Walter Moberly, *The Crisis in the University* (London, 1951); Basil A. Yeaxlee, *Religion and the Growing Mind* (London, 1952); Howard Lowry, *The Mind's Adventure* (Philadelphia, 1950); and Cornelius Jaarsma, *Fundamentals in Christian Education* (Grand Rapids, Mich., 1953).

For the Roman Catholic point of view the basic writings of St. Thomas Aquinas provide an almost endless source of ideas and background. Particularly important are the writings by Aquinas on the nature of man, on education and the teacher, and on human knowledge. These subjects are dealt with at length in the *Summa Theologica*.

Jacques Maritain, possibly Catholicism's most eminent authority on Aquinas, is considered an outstanding guide for our understanding of the Catholic outlook. *Man and the State* (Chicago, 1951) has been heavily drawn upon. Other works by Maritain which are considered significant to this section are *Education at the Crossroads* (New Haven, 1943), *Science and Wisdom* (London, 1940), and *Christianity and Democracy* (New York, 1945).

Other important references include Frederick Copleston, *A History of Philosophy* (Westminster, Md., 1950), Vol. II; M. C. D'Arcy (ed.), *Selected Writings of Thomas Aquinas* (New York, 1939); F. J. C. Hearnshaw, *Medieval Contributions to Modern Civilization* (New York, 1949); Hoxie N. Fairchild (ed.), *Religious Perspectives in College Teaching* (New York, 1952); Vergilius Ferm, *The Protestant Credo* (New York, 1953); Christian Gauss (ed.), *The Teaching of Religion in American Higher Education* (New York, 1951); Paul Blanshard, *Communism, Democracy and Catholic Power* (Boston, 1951); Gustaf Aulén, *The Faith of the Christian Church* (Philadelphia, 1948); Werner Jaeger, *Humanism and Theology* (Milwaukee, 1943); *A Monument to St. Augustine, Essays* (London, 1930); H. Richard Niebuhr, *Christ and Culture* (New York, 1951); R. P. Phillips, *Modern Thomistic Philosophy* (Westminster, Md., 1948), Vol. II; John Wild, *Introduction to Realistic Philosophy* (New York, 1948).

Articles

Luther A. Weigle is one of the noted authorities on problems of the relationship of religion to education. *Vital Speeches* carries one of his addresses on this subject, entitled "The Crisis of Religion in Education," XX (1953), 147-49. Other articles referring to this same problem are: Charles P. Taft, "Religion in the Public Schools," in *The Christian Century,* LXIX (1952), 944-46; Warren E. Gauerke, "Religion and the Public Schools: Some Legal Problems," in *School and Society,* LXXV (1952), 401-404; Paul Elbin, "Religion in State Schools," in *The Christian Century,* LXIX (1952), 1061-63; and M. Searle Bates, "Crisis in Catholic Columbia," in *The Christian Century,* LXXI (1954), 786-88.

Index

Activity, criticism of pragmatic emphasis, 43
Adler, Mortimer, 50, 64
Aquinas, Thomas, 49, 129, 130, 132, 136, 137
Aristotle, 38, 41, 46, 48, 49, 50, 56, 61, 66
Augustine, 145, 157
Authority: ecclesiastical, 2; revolt against, 6; classical concept, 39-40; reconstructionist views, 84, 101; Roman Catholic concept, 118-19; Reformation and Thomistic contrasts, 135-37, 139-41, 185-88; Reformation and pragmatic contrasts, 149-50

Babbitt, Irving, 68
Baillie, John, 157
Barth, Karl, 145, 146, 156
Boethius, 133
Brameld, Theodore, 83, 84, 85, 93
Bright, John, 190
Brunner, Emil, 146, 147, 149, 150, 151, 180, 181
Bunche, Ralph, 174

Calvin, John, 90, 146
Capitalism: critique of, 76-77; presently declining, 80
Childs, John, 149
Church and State: problem in education, 113-15; Roman Catholic view, 119-21; Reformation emphasis, 121-24; Protestant dilemma, 125, 176-77, 188; conflicting views, 142-43, 185-88; basis for common ground in conflict, 178-85; new interpretation, 195-98
Collectivism: inevitable, 76-77; and planning, 104; Reformation critique of, 146; its dangers in education, 171
Comenius, 87
Comte, Auguste, 23
Consciousness, the view of William James, 12-15
Contemplation, classical emphasis, 42-43
Counts, George, 81, 91

Crisis: in modern society, 96-97, 144-45, 179-80; in reference to faiths in education, 159-60

Darwin, Charles, 21, 23
Determinism, classical critique of, 55
Demiashkevich, Michael, 82
Democracy: pragmatic concept, 8; in education, 20; as related to pragmatic emphasis on fellowship, 32; classical concept, 41-42; social democracy, 80-81, 105; as a religion, 86; and the teacher, 105
Dewey, John, 3, 4, 7, 8, 24, 26, 28, 54, 78, 79, 80, 81, 82, 87, 88, 90, 91, 169
Discipline: critique of pragmatic concept, 59; classical emphasis, 59-60; reconstructionist view, 101-102

Economics, significance to education, 77-78
Emotions, important in reconstructionist emphasis, 93
Equalitarianism: critique of, 42, 71; reconstructionist emphasis, 91-92; Reformation view, 172-73
Evil: Greek concept, 49-50; pragmatic view, 31; reconstructionist idea of, 90-91, 95; Thomistic version, 131-32; Reformation concept, 132-34; communal significance, 141-42; Reformation and reconstructionist comparison, 154-55; prevents utopian hope, 168
Evolution: of the concept of responsibility, 23-24; as related to experience, 26
Experience: relation to truth, 5; definition by William James, 13-15; central to pragmatism, 26-27

Family, and education, 117-18, 165-67, 179-82
Fellowship: pragmatic emphasis, 31-32; classical view, 68-69
Field theory, as applied to personality, 94
Finney, Ross, 84, 95
Freedom: and intelligence, 30-31; Greek concept, 47; reconstructionist idea of, 100

377.2

R 763e

Date Due			
APR 3	1957		